GW00643267

Pride of Perth

Other books by Jack House

How to Clean an Elephant
Down the Clyde
Scotland for Fun
Square Mile of Murder
The Glory of Scotland – No 1 The West
The Glory of Scotland – No 2 The East
The Heart of Glasgow
Pavement in the Sun
Glasgow Old and New
Portrait of the Clyde
The Lang Toun

Frontispiece: The Coat of Arms of Arthur Bell & Sons
Limited

NUNC ET SEMPER

TO ALL AND SUNDRY,

Whom These Presents Do or May Concern, We, Sir Francis James Grant, Knight Commander of the Royal Victorian Order, Doctor of Laws, Lord Lyon King of Arms, Send Greeting:~ Whereas ARTHUR BELL AND SONS, Limited, Distillers, Perth, Scotland, having by Petition unto Us of date the Twenty~ Sixth day of May last, Shewn :~ THAT the business was founded in the year 1825 by Mr. T. R. Sandeman. After 1837 it was carried on by Mr. James Roy and later by Roy and Miller. In 1851 Mr. Arthur Bell entered the firm which then became known as Roy and Bell: THAT from 1862-65 the designation of the firm was Bell and Sandeman: THAT from 1865 till 1895 the business was conducted by Mr. Arthur Bell, who in the latter year admitted his sons into partnership and the firm took its name of Arthur Bell and Sons : THAT since the year 1922 the firm has been a Company registered under the Companies Acts under the name of Arthur Bell and Sons, Limited, having its registered Office at Number 11, Victoria Street, Perth, Scotland. AND the petition having Prayed that We would Grant Our Licence & Authority unto the said Company to bear and use such Ensigns Armorial as might be found suitable and according to the Laws of Arms : KNOW YE, therefore, that We have Devised and Do by These Presents Assign, Ratify and Confirm unto the said ARTHUR BELL AND SONS Limited the following Ensigns Armorial as depicted upon the margin hereof & matriculated of even date with These Presents upon the forty~third folio of the Thirty~fifth Volume of Our Public Register of All Arms and Bearings in Scotland, Videlicet :~ Vert, a bell Or. Above the shield is placed an helmet of befitting Degree with a Mantling Vert doubled Or, and on a Wreath of the Liveries is set for Crest:~ the sun rising Or. On a Compartment below the shield with this Motto~ NUNC ET SEMPER are set for Supporters~ two lions Gules, armed and langued Azure. In Testimony whereof These Presents are subscribed by Us and the Seal of Our Office is Affixed hereto at Edinburgh on the Twenty~fifth day of June in the Ninth Year of the Reign of Our Sovereign Lord George the Sixth, by the Grace of God, of Great Britain, Ireland and the British Dominions beyond the Seas, King, Defender of the Faith, Emperor of India etc., and in the Year of Our Lord One Thousand Nine Hundred and forty~five.

Francis J Grant
Lyon

Pride
of
Perth

The Story of Arthur Bell & Sons Ltd.
Scotch Whisky Distillers

Jack House

Hutchinson Benham, London

Hutchinson Benham Ltd
3 Fitzroy Square, London W1

An imprint of the Hutchinson Group

London Melbourne Sydney Auckland
Wellington Johannesburg and agencies
throughout the world

First published 1976
© Arthur Bell and Sons Ltd 1976

Designed and produced by Hutchinson Benham

Set in Monotype Scotch Roman
Printed in Great Britain by The Anchor Press Ltd
and bound by Wm Brendon & Son Ltd
both of Tiptree, Essex

ISBN 0 09 127320 X

Contents

Colour Plates

The Whisky man from Perth

On a fine day in the spring of 1845 a horseman cantered easily into a little village in the Highlands. He was a fresh-faced, burly young man and his arrival caused some excitement at the inn, which stood at one end of the village while the kirk faced it at the other.

'Father!' called the innkeeper's daughter as she saw the horseman. 'Here comes Mr Bell, the whisky man from Perth.'

The innkeeper came out to greet his visitor and took him into the wee room at the back which did duty for an office and where they sat over a dram.

'A nice quiet journey?' asked the innkeeper, an elderly man who had kept his howff for nigh on thirty years.

'Yes, indeed,' replied Arthur Bell. 'And why not?'

'You wouldn't ask that if you had seen the old days,' said the innkeeper. 'Your banker in Perth is Mr Stewart of the Bank of Scotland. Is that right?'

Arthur Bell agreed that it was so. 'Well,' said the innkeeper impressively, 'do you know that Mr Stewart still has his pistol to deal with highwaymen?'

The idea of encountering a highwayman had never occurred to Arthur Bell. He was the traveller for a firm of wine and spirits dealers in the city of Perth, and his job was not only to take orders but to collect the money due to the firm by its customers. For three months of every year he travelled Scotland by train and coach, where that was possible, but sometimes on horseback when there was no other way.

'Aye, well,' said the innkeeper, 'your friend Patrick Stewart told me that he started with the Bank of Scotland's Perth branch when it was opened in 1784. At the very time he took on the job, the Bank brought out a rule that, when a clerk took remittances to branches, he must carry a loaded pistol, ready to fire on any high-wayman who tried to hold him up. Mr Stewart didn't have to do this kind of work at first but, when it came to travelling as an Agent for the Bank, he bought a good second-hand pistol for four guineas, and the Bank of Scotland paid for it. And he's still got it today – twenty-eight years after he bought it.'

Arthur Bell decided that he would look with even more respect upon Patrick Gilbert Stewart, manager of the Bank of Scotland in Perth. And he breathed a silent prayer of thanks that highwaymen were no longer infesting his visiting grounds of the quiet roads of the Highlands.

The traveller's Highland tour was an arduous three months, but he enjoyed it. In any case, he had made up his mind that he was going to be more than just a traveller in the firm. Not that it was much of a firm at the moment. Indeed, it consisted of Mr Sandeman, the owner, a clerk named James Roy, a cellarman, a boy, and Arthur Bell. It had gone quietly on since the business was started by Thomas R. Sandeman twenty years earlier.

Thomas Sandeman was related to the Sandeman family of Oporto and he knew something of the wine and spirits trade. But it must have taken some courage for him to start his shop in the Kirkgate of Perth, for the city was having hard times in 1825.

Perth is a proud city and still remembers that it was the capital of Scotland until King James III transferred the seat of monarchy to Edinburgh in 1482. And Perth can trace its history back to the days of the Romans, for General Agricola established a camp there. At the beginning of the thirteenth century Perth was a flourishing city when Glasgow was a mere village in the shadow of its cathedral. At that time the Abbot Necham of Exeter wrote:

Great Tay, through Perth, through towns, through country flies,
Perth the whole kingdom with her wealth supplies.

During the eighteenth century the principal manufacture in Perth was linen and the Perth merchants dealt directly with the Continent. In 1797 there were no fewer than forty-six watermills within four miles of Perth, all engaged in bleaching and printing linen and cotton. Then came the slump and even the Duke of

The Kirk of St John, Perth

Wellington's victory at Waterloo couldn't bring the citizens of Perth out of the doldrums.

By 1825 things had improved only a little. The population of Perth was just under 20,000 and one report said, 'The poor in Perth are numerous.' It wasn't an altogether auspicious time to start a new business, but Thomas Sandeman felt he could rely on the Oporto Sandemans because that business had been founded by George Sandeman of Perth in 1790. He opened his shop in the Kirkgate of the city, on the south side of the ancient Church of St John, famous for its bells. A contemporary refers to the oldest bell, 'a little skelloch [shrill] bell' cast in the year 1400, St John the Baptist's bell of 1506, and a renowned chime of large bells. By the time Arthur Bell came into the firm, he must have felt thoroughly at home.

Thomas Sandeman soon found that the shop in the Kirkgate was not big enough for all his activities. He was dealing not only in whisky but in a large range of wines, beers, and even tea. This seems remarkable today, but tea came under the heading of bonded goods and was as liable to excise duty as the alcoholic items. So, needing more space, especially for the storing of casks and bottles, Thomas Sandeman proposed to some of the other wine merchants and whisky dealers in Perth that they should buy an old granary in the Speygate and convert it into a warehouse. He said that this warehouse 'was not taken for our private use only, but for the accommodation at the lowest possible rent of all who might choose to lodge wines and spirits therein. We are willing to allow such wine and spirit merchants as may be so disposed to participate in any profit which may from time to time result from the speculation, upon condition of their agreeing to pay a share of any loss.'

Thomas Sandeman took on a clerk by the name of James Roy, and Roy gradually became more of a partner than an employee. They did a retail as well as a wholesale business and Sandeman went out for the county type of people who lived in and around Perth. He wrote to Lord Kinnoul, 'Should Lord Kinnoul, at any future time, think of making trial of my Port wine, I feel very great confidence in recommending to his Lordship the Wine I receive from my friend, Messrs Sandeman of Oporto, who has for some time past held the most extensive stock of any House in the country.'

Perth from the south, showing the pumping station
(round tower), now the Tourist Information Board

That was one end of the scale. The other is shown in a note which accompanied a delivery of spirits to John Alexander, the owner of an inn at Meigle in the north of Perthshire. Sandeman wrote, 'I shall not charge you more than eight shillings, although that price does not pay me, and I beg you not to mention it to others whom I must charge higher.' Which is one way of implying to a customer that he's getting value for money.

By 1837 the business was doing well. Thomas Sandeman had even gone outside the wine and spirits trade and started agencies in iron, insurance and spinning. His profit for his main business came to almost £1000, which was a good result on sales of £5500. But in that year Thomas Sandeman died, and the business was taken over by James Roy, the clerk. Eventually Roy brought in a man named Miller as a partner and the time came when, needing a traveller, they engaged Arthur Bell. The man of the future had arrived.

It was about this time that the famous Temperance reformer, Father Matthew, was stumping the country, speaking on the evils

The Temperance leader, the Very Revd Theobald Matthew (1790–1856), administering the Temperance pledge

of strong drink. Teetotal societies were springing up everywhere and 'signing the pledge' became a popular thing to do. This, combined with another slump in trade which hit Perth as well as the rest of the country, resulted in a very definite fall in the sale of whisky and other spirits, although, strangely enough, the sale of beer and wines went up. But the profits went down, and were actually lower than they were in the time of Thomas Sandeman.

Miller left the partnership in 1851 and Roy immediately asked his energetic young salesman to become a partner. The firm became Roy and Bell. They were still operating from the same shop and cellar in the Kirkgate, and the staff had not grown over the years. There were the working partners, though, when he did become a partner, Arthur Bell cut down his travelling and debt collecting considerably. They had a clerk to do the office work, a cellarman to do the bottling down below, and a boy who delivered orders by pushing a handcart around the town. When he wasn't trundling his handcart, the boy was expected to act as salesman in the shop, for plenty of wines and spirits were sold over the counter.

Since Arthur Bell had decided that, henceforward, he would travel no farther north than Kirriemuir, a new traveller was needed, and he brought in one of his nephews, T. R. Sandeman, a son of the founder of the business. This gave Arthur Bell more time to interest himself in the blending of whisky. There were many small singly-owned distilleries in Scotland at that time, and Arthur Bell went round them looking for quality. Sometimes the distillery was not much more than a large farm, but the farmer was able to produce a fine whisky.

By this time Arthur Bell was working out his own blends from the various malts and the grain whiskies. What he was out for was a blend which would reproduce the qualities of the original whiskies. And he was thinking of selling these high-class blends south of the border. It was time that the English were educated in the taste of really good Scotch whisky.

Like all blenders, Arthur Bell was secretive about his methods. One Perth business man wrote and asked him what was in his best whisky, and Bell wrote back, 'I do not usually give the mixture of my whiskies, but may mention that the best is made in Banffshire's Glenlivet district, and the other is Pitlochry and Stirlingshire whiskies.'

One strong trait in Arthur Bell's character, and one that remained with him to the end of his life, was his horror of debt, particularly other people's debts to him and his firm. He wasn't too keen on the public house trade, because some publicans were not too ready to pay their accounts. It's surprising how many small, and not so small, firms went to the wall in Victorian days because of bad debts.

Arthur was stern with customers who were lagging in their payments. He wrote to a Mrs Keir of Pitlochry, 'Mr Bell was much surprised and disappointed that Mrs Keir did not settle this old balance with Mr Sandeman and he hopes she will remit it without delay as such long credit eats up all the profits in the business, the usual credit on whisky is three months (not a year).'

That's bad enough, but how about this billet doux to Mrs Rodger of Auchtermuchty?

Madam,

On 14th February last you called at my office and got one bottle whisky and two bottles brandy value 8/3 promising to call and pay it on a fortnight after. I was under the presumption that you were a lady and would keep your promise, although a stranger to me.

If I do not hear from you before Friday first I will have a different opinion of your character and will take steps accordingly.'

The handcart used by Bell's messenger boy to deliver orders to customers in Perth

That must have put the cat among the pigeons in Auchtermuchty.

Then there were the rude and licentious soldiery, for Perth had a barracks in those days. Roy and Bell supplied the regimental messes in the barracks and also officers and N.C.O.s who wanted to open an account. Arthur Bell didn't worry about the individual accounts because, if some junior officer didn't pay, all the firm had to do was get in touch with his commanding officer. The mere threat of this was enough to make the offender pay up promptly.

Even the messes were sometimes at fault. Arthur Bell had a high regard for the 79th Foot, who paid their bills regularly. But he wrote to Her Majesty's 14th Light Dragoons that 'we have supplied many messes but *yours* is the first that has not paid us'.

Despite Arthur Bell's preoccupation with bad debts, the business of Roy and Bell was doing well. One reason for the increase, particularly in the selling of whisky, was the development of railways in Scotland. In Arthur's days as a traveller, as we have seen, a great deal of arduous journeying went into his spring safari. The new railway lines spreading up and across the Highlands made an enormous difference, not only to the new traveller, young Sandeman, but to the despatch and delivery of whisky and other potables to customers all over the country.

The coming of the railways also affected the supplies of whisky to Roy and Bell, but they could have taken more advantage of the opportunities to buy whisky from the distillers. They seem to have been a thought canny and the time was to come when they would be caught out because of that. Whisky today is only sold when it has matured – it must be at least three years old. In the fifties and sixties of the last century it was frequently sold new or from six months to a year old. But the public taste for mature whisky was growing, and the partners in Perth should have realized that it was worth their while to build up a stock of good malt whiskies for blending purposes.

True, Arthur Bell on his own later chose Glenlivet and other fine Highland malts as a base to blend from, but while he was still in partnership with Roy they used only one Highland malt and that was Edradour, near Pitlochry. They bought their whisky, both malt and grain, from Lowland distilleries, which were cheaper than the Highland malts.

Chancellors of the Exchequer have always been famous for choosing whisky as a whipping boy. There is a known case where a

Excise duty, 1723

Chancellor put an extra tax on whisky to help the Government finance a small war in India. We assume, of course, that the duty on whisky has always been at a similar level for all the countries of the United Kingdom. But this was not the case in the middle of the nineteenth century. Then the duty on whisky in Scotland was not as high as the duty in England, nor Ireland when it comes to that. The Government, however, decided on 'equalization' and the excise duty, which had been four shillings and eightpence per proof gallon in Scotland went up first to six shillings, then to eight shillings, and in five years had equalized with England at ten shillings. In that time the consumption of whisky in Scotland fell by nearly a half.

Roy and Bell were completely unprepared for the rise in duty to ten shillings a proof gallon. They hadn't enough duty-paid stock to meet their orders, and that meant they had to raise their prices immediately. Naturally, they suffered for their lack of foresight, but at least it made Arthur Bell all the keener on expanding his whisky business outside Scotland.

Whisky was becoming more and more important to the firm. When the excise duty on tea was abandoned by the Government, Roy and Bell gradually stopped selling the cup that cheers but doesn't inebriate. They were still selling wines and brandies and

B

port, but they were no longer worrying about keeping up their stocks of beer and stout and cider, except for regular orders which, Arthur Bell felt fairly confident, wouldn't include any bad debts!

Perhaps it was all these worries which caused James Roy, the senior partner, to decide on retiring in 1862. The partnership was dissolved, but Roy kept some money in the firm. Arthur Bell immediately invited his nephew, T. R. Sandeman the traveller, to join him in partnership. This seemed a good idea, because young Sandeman brought £2597 into the business, whereas Arthur Bell's investment was £1949. But it turned out to be a sad mistake.

Young Sandeman was a bright boy and, like many another traveller at that time, had picked up various agencies for firms who couldn't afford a full-time traveller. This wasn't in the least unusual, and Arthur Bell would certainly know the practice existed because he had fixed up his first agent in London, who was a traveller working for the Canon Brewery there. The Canon Brewery was one of the southern firms which supplied Roy and Bell, and now Bell and Sandeman, with beer.

Sandeman found that his extra-mural activities were more profitable than just working as a partner in the Perth firm. He was inclined to neglect the business which meant so much to Arthur Bell. Not only that, but he was careless about his personal accounts and inclined to charge various expenses up to the firm which he should have paid himself. We know that Arthur Bell was meticulous about money and, when he discovered that Sandeman had bought a box of cigars for himself and a portrait for his mother and charged them to Bell and Sandeman, Bell was outraged. The sum was only £8, but it was the principle of the thing that irked Arthur Bell.

Next he found that Sandeman had charged £12 for the hire of a horse and gig, which he had used entirely on his own agency business. When Bell taxed Sandeman with this, the younger partner refused absolutely to pay for the hire.

Arthur Bell, like most Victorians a great letter-writer, penned an epistle to his erring partner, in the course of which he said:

You remember you and I agreed that we should each be liable for our own accidents happening, either to horse or gig, but those have occurred when travelling about your own private affairs unconnected with the business, but as I gave Ritchie (the hirer of the horse and gig) no instructions to keep your

account separate from the firm's, of course he now looks to me
for payment and, as I have no intention of going to law with
him in regard to a debt due by you, if I cannot recover it from
you I must pay it myself and be the loser however unjustly,
and can only say I expected more honourable treatment at
your hands.

Be so good as to let me know what answer I shall give. I
may remark that I am sorry to see you write in such an
unfriendly strain, as I am ignorant of having given any cause
for it. I believe I have always acted most justly towards you,
and am only asking for the same in return.

Sandeman did not even reply to this epistle, and Arthur Bell
wrote to him an even stronger letter. It said, in part –

Since writing you I have felt so much hurt at your evident
intention of saddling me with £20.11.6 of your debt, with which
I have nothing earthly to do, that I intend resisting payment of
Ritchie's claim against you, which will bring an action before
the Sheriff, in which your behaviour will be fully exposed and,
as Ritchie tells me he has plenty of evidence to show how unfit
you were to be entrusted with horse and gigs, I don't see how
the Sheriff can give any other decision but against you, but
before doing anything further in this matter I intend laying
the correspondence before Messrs Roy and Spears *if I do not
receive an immediate remittance* for the above amount.

Some time passed and Arthur Bell, against his own feelings, felt
he must go ahead with the action against Sandeman. But suddenly
the erring partner sent his cheque for £20 11s 6d. Arthur Bell had
the second last word in the stramash. In yet another letter he
expressed 'regret that you did not clear up these matters before you
left, as it has been very painful for me to receive such communica-
tions as you have lately thought proper to send to me'.

The last word went to T. R. Sandeman who announced that, as
far as he was concerned, the partnership was over and he must
have his £2597 back. As a man of honour, Arthur Bell saw that
Sandeman was paid out right away. And then he sat in his shop in
the Kirkgate and contemplated a gloomy future.

Family Affair

ARTHUR BELL was still only a middle-aged man, but he was the patriarch of a large family. And, in his Victorian way of honour and rectitude, he regarded it as his duty to look after any member of the family who needed help. So the money which came in from the whisky business was of supreme importance to him.

One of the reasons why young Sandeman had behaved as he did was that he thought the profits were too small. He didn't appear to take into account the fact that, owing to his own laxity, the effort that the firm had made to get into the London market had failed, and that they were faced with Arthur Bell's bête noire – bad debts by the dozen.

The profit of Bell and Sandeman's in their last year of working together was £1925, and that was not much for the two partners, especially when one of them was looking after so many relations. Then, at one fell stroke, the capital of the firm had been reduced from £5253 to £2656 because of Sandeman's withdrawal.

Arthur Bell had £1949 in the firm and his old partner, James Roy, had £667. The remaining £40 comprised £30 from the Roy and Bell partnership and a loan of £10 from the Central Bank. The first thing that Arthur Bell did was to deny himself any profit at all from the year's business. Then he sank his pride and approached two elderly lady friends of the Bell family, the Misses Duff. They advanced £1305. But the biggest change of all in his business out-look was when he went to the Central Bank and raised the capital the Bank had in the company from £10 to £2097. This went so much against the grain that, when he was able to pay out the Central Bank five years later, he never again used this form of finance.

High Street, Perth

The Bell family drained much of Arthur's resources. However canny he was about his daily business, he seemed never to be able to say them nay. He gave money to Robert Bell to help him in his civil engineering course. When James Bell in Glasgow wanted to be a dental surgeon, Arthur gave him a loan to tide him over his training and set him up in practice, with the proviso that this money was 'never to be claimed until he is quite able to pay'. Elliot Bell wanted to seek his fortune in Canada, while Imrie Bell's goal was New Zealand. Arthur Bell paid the passage for each of them. He helped his three sisters, Anna, Marion and Isabella by investing his money in the firm for them.

Doubtless Arthur Bell got some gratification from these gifts and loans, but there was one which brought only misfortune. John Bell came to him with a proposal that there was money to be made as an importer of guano fertilizer in Leith. He put his case so convincingly that Arthur made him a loan of £2000 to establish the business. But John Bell had miscalculated things. He had not, apparently, realized that there were remarkable fluctuations in supplies of guano from Peru. And he appears to have ignored the fact that there was an almost total monopoly of guano imports by London agents. Not only that, but already as he had started business, guano was going out of fashion as a manure and was being replaced by other manufactured artificial fertilizers.

It was only a matter of time before events overtook John Bell. His business failed in 1867. Some time after that, he died in mysterious circumstances. Many people thought he had committed suicide. Naturally, it was Arthur Bell who saw to the winding up of John's guano firm and it was Arthur Bell who took over the responsibility for John's wife and family.

As far as his own business was concerned, Arthur Bell was still trying to salvage something from the wreck of his hopes in London. He had started well ahead of the rest of the Scotch whisky trade, but seemed to get nowhere. As far back as 1855 he had offered whisky to a firm in England, without success. He appointed, as far as is known, the first Scotch whisky agent in London in 1862, getting him through the kind offices of the family friend, Sandeman and Company.

Arthur Bell was a man of strong opinions, and he did not see any reason why the Londoners should not appreciate the Scotch whisky that the Scots liked. It never occurred to him that people close on five hundred miles away might have different tastes. His first agent, a Mr Young, reported back that London people thought that Bell's whisky had too heavy a taste. Mr Bell was astonished. He wrote back right away –

Your friends do not seem to be aware that the finer whiskies in Scotland are only made at 11 to 11.6 o.p. and that, when kept a couple of years, they fall in strength at least three per cent. We do not usually send out our whisky to customers who are particular as to quality until it is of that age, but if your friends value the strength more than the quality, we must just send them new whisky.

Despite this criticism and Bell's reply, things were going modestly well, but at the end of the first year of the London agency, Arthur Bell was writing:

I have been expecting to see or hear from Mr Young as he promised but have been disappointed and, as the few customers he got for us may now be going elsewhere for their whisky and we are unwilling to make a new arrangement with Mr Young in the way he proposed to Mr Sandeman, we would feel much obliged by your proposing to any party whom you think suitable in every respect to carry on the agency in the same way as Mr Young did. I may mention that there is still owing to us by Mr Young £29. 0. 10. overdue.

Arthur Bell got a change of agents, but no joy with it. Sandeman's suggested a Mr Schofield. Within four months Bell was writing to Sandeman's that 'Mr Schofield is sleeping'. The crunch for Arthur Bell came in October 1864. The amount outstanding in London accounts was £113. Schofield had reported no new orders for three months. Bell asked for action from Sandeman's, and they discovered that Schofield had already received the £113 but had done nothing about it. Bell threatened legal action and got a little of his money back. In the meantime he had his final quarrel with his partner and wrote to Schofield in June 1865, 'that my partnership with Mr Sandeman is dissolved and, as I intend to withdraw my London agency, I will feel particularly obliged by your collecting the accounts and remitting them to me *without delay.*'

But this didn't work either. Schofield was sacked and another agent brought in, but Arthur Bell complained of him, 'he only gets orders for small quantities of whisky in jars. I have not yet received a penny from him.'

The trouble, though apparently Bell didn't see it, was that a man might be a very good salesman but a bad collector of accounts. He tried a fourth agent in London, James Ruston, a traveller for the Canon Brewery. Ruston asked Arthur Bell for a list of his London customers and Bell sent him twenty-five names, almost all of hotels and public houses. Included among them was the Goat and Star in Piccadilly, the Red Cow in Smithfield, and the Clothworkers' Arms in Islington. It was not a very impressive list and Arthur Bell wasn't even sure that it was still valid, 'it being some years ago since some of them purchased'.

But Ruston, like the others, was a man of straw. He didn't produce a single order from London and Arthur Bell gave up his attempt to capture some of the London market in 1871. If orders came his way from London, he was glad to supply them. But he made no overt attempt to seek new business there. Instead he decided to concentrate more strongly on his Scottish sales and to explore the possibilities of the export trade. He was fairly happy with his profit situation. He was making a clear profit of about £2000 a year. And now that he was the sole partner, that seemed to him to be quite a respectable sum, especially when he compared it with his rivals in the whisky trade.

He must have felt reasonably confident about his business position because he now found time to embark on one of his campaigns. Arthur Bell was a great campaigning man and he passed the trait on to the son who succeeded him, Arthur Kinmond Bell. This campaign of 1871 was to establish a regular size of bottle for spirits and wines.

On 23 March 1871, he wrote to his M.P., Arthur Kinnaird:

I beg to call your attention to the necessity there is for a Bill being passed by Parliament that bottles should be made of one uniform size throughout the United Kingdom.

Whilst all other articles of consumption are sold by weight or by measure, wines, spirits and malt liquors are generally sold by the bottle, or dozen bottles, which bottle ought to represent one sixth of a gallon, and the half bottle one twelfth, or in other words six of the one or twelve of the other, when corked, should contain exactly one gallon, but the fact is there are at least three sizes of bottles manufactured, viz. six, six and a third, and six and a half to the gallon, which operates very injuriously on those of the public who receive their liquors in the smaller bottles, and on those of the Trade who use only the largest size. . . .

To remedy this grievance the Government has simply to adopt the plan successfully pursued by the Emperor Napoleon in France, by appointing Inspectors to each Bottle work in the Kingdom, whose duty would be to pass only those bottles of the legal size, and to cause all others to be thrown back into the furnace, thus every year would diminish the numbers of smaller bottles in circulation until, even during our lifetime, we would see only one uniform size in use, and quality alone would be the criterion of the value of their contents instead of, as now, quantity as well as quality having to be considered.

Yours faithfully, Arthur Bell.

1   The water used in the distilling of Scotch whisky,
perhaps the most important contributory factor to
the quality of the end product

11   *A view of Perth and the river Tay*, by J. L. Cranstone

III   Kincarrathie House, Perth

IV   The Gannochy housing estate, Perth, built in the 1920s by A. K. Bell

Now this seems to be an eminently sensible suggestion, but Parliament doesn't always work on sensible suggestions. The House of Commons at this time was debating a Licensing Bill and the general opinion was that they shouldn't countenance side issues. Anyway, as a good M.P., Arthur Kinnaird replied from 1 Pall Mall East –

My dear Sir,
I have thought it best to put myself in communication with the Chancellor of the Exchequer on the subject of your letter, and I hope in a day or two again to write to you.
Ever truly yours,
A. Kinnaird.

This was followed by an exchange of letters of a style which must be familiar to anyone who has had to deal with Government departments. Arthur Bell kept to his point, however. He said in one of his letters: 'I cannot understand how the appointment by Government of Inspectors to each bottle work can be considered a greater restraint than that of Excise Officers at Distilleries, Breweries and Maltings. In the one case it would be to protect the Public, and in the other case it is for the protection of the Revenue, and the expense of inspection could be defrayed by a Licence Tax on Bottle makers, as is already the case on Distillers, Brewers, Wine Merchants and others.'

Arthur Bell ended his letter by saying, 'As I observed that *The Times* contained a leading article on the subject on Thursday last, I shall feel obliged by receiving your permission to send a copy of this correspondence to the Editor for publication.'

This put the cat among the pigeons. A high official of the Board of Trade wrote back to Arthur Bell saying that the whole correspondence was private and should not be published in the Press. Mr Bell had the last word, however. He wrote to his M.P., 'I am sorry to see that the Government has not had the courage "to take the bull by the horns".'

Naturally, Arthur Bell in his day could not have envisaged a situation where his firm would actually control its own bottle supply. But that is the case today, when Bell's own a bottle-making company in London and control their supplies.

As you may imagine from the bottle correspondence, Arthur Bell was an important figure in Perth by this time. He knew all the best people and was a person of some consequence. It was all the more mortifying to him when the Excise brought a prosecution against him for fraud.

He himself had invoked the aid of the law on more than one occasion. Indeed, there was a case not long before this when he had had trouble with an innkeeper in Glenlyon to whom he had lent money. This was quite a common practice among distillers in those days, but Bell, with his horror of bad debts, had set his face against it. However, for the first time he had lent money to the Glenlyon innkeeper. When the time came for repayment, no money was forthcoming. Not only that, but Arthur Bell discovered that the Glenlyon man was actually getting his whisky from another distiller, which was certainly adding insult to injury.

He wrote sternly to the innkeeper:

You wrote me on 21st August last that if I would give you till Martinmas, you would then send me some money and that, if not, I was not to spare you, and now you insult me by sending a single pound as part payment of the prefixed large amount (£41.11.10), three pounds being all I have received during the whole year.

You must consider me a great simpleton if I am content with that paltry sum, and knowing that you have received £41.11.10 in addition. I have now to tell you that I will not be content unless you pay me by instalments as you proposed, say £2 every month, which is little enough to ask from you, and I think the least you can do in addition is to take your supplies of whisky from me, paying cash as you get it, and I trust you will see the necessity of agreeing to this.

But apparently the Glenlyon man didn't see the necessity, and Arthur Bell engaged a lawyer in Perth to write to him 'and threaten the terrors of the law if a payment to account is not at once sent'.

It was one thing, though, to be on the right side of the law, and quite another to be charged with fraud. What happened was that, in 1873, Arthur Bell made an arrangement with a malt distiller in Pitlochry (where Bell's Blair Athol distillery stands today) to sell his whisky as an agent. His idea was to push Connacher's malt in the Scottish market, particularly in Glasgow. He got one of his Sandeman nephews to do the selling, but young Fitzroy Sandeman found a lot of difficulty in persuading the Glasgow buyers to take

The Fair Maid's House, Perth

the Pitlochry whisky because the distillers in the West of Scotland
were keeping their prices low. Indeed, after five months of getting
nowhere, Fitzroy Sandeman gave up the job and went to a new one
in Exeter.

Arthur Bell decided to give up the Connacher agency, but
managed to get Charles Sandeman, Fitzroy's brother, to take it
over. So he gave Alexander Connacher notice that all would soon
be over between them. What he apparently didn't know was that
Connacher was fed up with the arrangement too because there was
so little money in it. The Pitlochry distiller decided to put this right
by working a fiddle. All he had to do was to falsify the Excise
permits on whisky deliveries, send out more malt whisky than the

amount on the permit, collect the difference and pocket the illegal profit.

Naturally, Arthur Bell did not know that Connacher had hatched his little plot. The first he heard was when the Excise charged Alexander Connacher and Arthur Bell jointly with making false returns. He was horrified. He consulted the M.P. for Perth and, on his advice, wrote to the Commissioners of Inland Revenue:

I am informed by your Honors' Supervisor here that it is your Honors' intention to institute proceedings against me for taking into stock a cask of whisky without having entered it into my stock book. I hope your Honors will reconsider the simple facts of the case and see how innocently I have been led into error.

Connacher sent me word that one of my casks lying in his bond was leaking, being in bad condition, and that he would pay duty on it at once and send it to me. A cask of whisky was delivered at my premises with apparently a permit underneath the address and all appeared correct, and a receipt was given to the Railway Carter as usual. But after the Carter had left, and when it was too late to refuse to take delivery, I found that instead of a permit being under the address card, there was only a railway delivery note.

I immediately returned this paper by post in a note to Connacher, requesting the permit to be sent in its place, copy of which and a subsequent note were given to your officers, as also the receipt for the full duty being paid by me.

Connacher afterwards called at my office (I think he said he had come from Glasgow) and said that his clerk must have mislaid my permit, but that he would see that it was sent when he went home, after which time I never heard from him, although I was always in expectation of him looking in at my office with the permit.

I would most respectfully but earnestly entreat your Honors to prevent such a case going into court on the following grounds. I have been upwards of 24 years in business here and I have never been in a Court of Justice as a defendant in any case whatever, and being prosecuted by the Excise may seriously affect my business.

I have never before taken delivery of spirits without a permit, and in this instance did so unknowingly.

My only mistake was in taking what I thought the simplest method of rectifying the distiller's apparent oversight by writing to the distiller instead of at once informing the Excise, which I trust your Honors will consider an error of judgment on my part into which I have innocently been led.

Of course, if I had had the slightest idea of it having been anything but an oversight of the distiller's clerk, I would not have lost a moment in communicating the circumstances to the Excise authorities.

I therefore entreat your Honors to remit any penalties I may have incurred, and I remain

> Your Honors' most obedient humble servant,
> Arthur Bell.

With this letter Bell enclosed a Certificate of Character, and the titles of the signatories speak for themselves. It read –

Mr Arthur Bell is one of the principal wine and spirit merchants in Perth and has conducted that business for upwards of 24 years past. He has all along borne a most excellent character and conducted his business in a regular and most satisfactory way and enjoys the respect and esteem of his fellow citizens.

We believe him to be incapable of attempting anything having the appearance of fraud and have no hesitation in recommending the Honorable Board of Inland Revenue to put implicit faith in his explanations in the foregoing memorial and to remit the penalties which he may have incurred:

Archd. McDonald	Lord Provost of Perth
Robert Robertson	Magistrate
John McArthur	Magistrate
James Wotherspoon	Magistrate
Archibald Burns	J.P. for Perthshire
Hugh Barclay	S.S. and J.P., Perthshire
Melville Jameson	Procurator Fiscal

As I say, this is an impressive list of signatories particularly the Lord Provost at the top and the Procurator Fiscal at the bottom. The Lord Provost is the Scottish equivalent of a Lord Mayor in

England, and the Procurator Fiscal is the official who collects the evidence in cases of law and decides whether they should go to court or not. Incidentally, the penalty demanded by the Excise authorities was a fine of £100.

Bell had sent his memorial and the certificate of character to his M.P., Sir William Stirling Maxwell, Bart., to be forwarded to the Commissioners of Inland Revenue but, after nearly two weeks had passed, and the Commissioners had made no reply, he wrote direct to them, sending copies of the memorial and certificate in case they had not been sent on by Sir William, and expressing the hope that they would countermand the instructions given for his prosecution. He added:

No doubt stringent clauses in the Excise Laws referable to my case were framed for the purpose of preventing or detecting fraud, and not for annoying and harassing honest traders, and in a case like mine, where no fraud on the Revenue was intended, and no benefit to myself could have been derived, your Honors may be assured that the annoyance I have felt at being summoned to appear like a criminal before a Justice of the Peace Court will be sufficient to prevent a recurrence of a similar mistake.

A reply from the Inland Revenue Office in Somerset House came within a day or two. It said that the prosecution 'will be stayed on your immediately paying to the Supervisor of Inland Revenue at Perth Compromise fine of Ten Pounds'.

Arthur Bell paid the £10 immediately, and then wrote yet another letter to the Commissioners, making his points all over again, and ending by 'hoping that your Honors may be pleased to order the Ten Pounds to be repaid to me'.

You might think he was being unnecessarily persistent (and so might the Commissioners!), but consider the effect upon him in Perth. He wrote to a friend, 'I feel very acutely about it being so widely known, and so much talked about. Everyone acquainted with the circumstances express much astonishment at the harsh treatment by the Excise, casting an apparent slur on my character, as if I had been in some way connected with Connacher's misdeeds, instead of being a victim of his deception.'

The last word in this saga came from Somerset House. The Secretary of the Board of Inland Revenue replied to Arthur Bell:

I am desired to remind you that it was your duty to have
entered the cask of spirits in question on the day you received
it, or informed the Revenue Officers that the spirits had arrived
without a permit and, by your failure to do so, you prevented
an earlier discovery of the Distiller's frauds.

Moreover, by your neglect to meet with the requirements of
the law, you rendered yourself liable to heavy penalties, and the
Board are of opinion that your case has been treated with
sufficient leniency.

They cannot accede to your present request.

Arthur Bell kept all the documents in the case for the rest of his
life and, right to the end, was ready to talk about the injustice done
to him by the Board of Inland Revenue.

At the time, however, one of the principal effects of the incident
was to make him suspicious of everybody except his friends. He
had a right, of course, to be suspicious in some quarters. Now that
his whisky was being sold in parts of Scotland where he had not
traded before, he found that the transport systems were plagued
with pilfering, which became as much an obsession to him as his
bad debts worry.

He wrote to the Loch Lomond Steam Boat Company, 'As in
almost every instance when I send whisky by your boats my cus-

The head of Loch Lomond, looking south

tomers complain of considerable quantities being abstracted, I am determined that such shall now be put a stop to, and that somebody will pay for it. I have therefore to inform you that, unless you remit me the 15/3, I will have the case tried against you in the Law Courts.'

The railway was every bit as bad for pilfering as the steam boats. Arthur Bell wrote of, 'Those wretched railways servants, at their old tricks again; thinking that one bottle from each case would not be missed, they have loosened the cord and nails and pressed up a board, replacing them as before, after abstracting the bottles.'

Yes, it was a sair fecht, as we say in Scotland. But I wouldn't have you think that Arthur Bell was always down in the dumps. He had an eye for the smaller things in life. He was not an extrovert, as so many of his whisky compatriots in Perth were at that time. He got his main enjoyment in his family life, and was proud of the way his two sons were growing up, for he had a notion to keep them in the family business.

He was a humane man too, as witness this letter which he wrote to a firm of carters in Glasgow. 'When your carter was as usual receiving goods today from me for the Railway Company, I had the curiosity to compare the food which he gave his horse with that which Messrs Cameron gave, his cart being also at my door, and I must say the latter was much more nourishing, a much larger proportion of corn being in his bag. In mercy to your poor horses you should look after their feeding.'

I wonder what the Glasgow carter said when he got that one!

3

Going out in the World

ARTHUR BELL was a typical Victorian, with all the virtues and some of the vices which characterized the Victorians. He had a sentimental – often too sentimental – regard for his family, he was over-worried about his respectability (as witness the Inland Revenue case), he had an abhorrence of bad debts, double dealing, and any kind of attack on property; but there was one side of his life from which he never deviated – he had an almost holy regard for the quality of the whisky he was producing. This, of course, has been one of the secrets, if secret it is, of Bell's success.

The really odd thing is that, while he was always striving to produce the perfect whisky (and it hurt him if his customers wanted a cheaper, and therefore inferior in his opinion, product), he didn't even put his own name on it. As far as we can discover, Arthur Bell never thought of putting his own brand name on the bottles, or selling his casks under a distinctive title. He had no trademark and no label. When a customer in Glasgow expressed his surprise about this, Arthur Bell replied, stating his philosophy as far as whisky was concerned. He said that thirty years in the trade had taught him:

that several fine whiskies blended together please the palates of a greater number of people than one whisky unmixed, consequently I have long adopted that practice, and never found it necessary to send out showcards but just allowed the qualities of my goods to *speak for themselves*.

The best whisky I sent you is a combination from seven different distilleries, and the cheaper is a blend of Highland and South Country Whiskies, and I am glad to hear they give satisfaction.

c

But events overtook Arthur Bell. Up until the great boom in whisky in 1890, the market fluctuated according to events which had nothing to do with distilling or blending. Strangely enough, the Franco-Prussian War seemed to help the sale of whisky, but the terrible collapse of the City of Glasgow Bank in 1878 was a catastrophe for the whisky men.

One of Bell's biggest problems was that his own bottling premises was the small cellar underneath the shop in the Kirkgate. It was quite inadequate when he went into the export trade and, though he got his export whisky bottled in such blending centres as Glasgow, Leith and Edinburgh, his home trade grew as well and the cellar became impossible. Up till then he had concentrated on casks rather than bottles of whisky, but now bottles were the thing – and bottles with proprietary labels on them. He was being irresistibly moved towards providing his own label on his own bottle. And one of the points which helped him to decide on this was the fact that unscrupulous whisky retailers could sell his cask whisky under any name they liked.

While he was having all these problems, his export business was building up slowly. The first enquiry came from an old customer who was now living abroad, but the second and third came from hotel proprietors in Italy who were Scots and had Scottish visitors who still wanted to taste the wine of their own country. A Miss Dick, who ran L'Hôtel des Anglais in San Remo, asked for a supply of Bell's best Scotch. Arthur Bell sent his finest whisky to San Remo. It was dearer than the blend he sold at home but the price didn't matter. The taste did, and Miss Dick got in touch with her friend, Miss McPherson, who ran the Hôtel Britannique in Naples and told her the good news. Miss McPherson put in an order but, owing to shipping trouble, it didn't arrive until the tourist season was over.

Arthur Bell recorded, 'I was in hopes this would be the commencement of many future shipments to Naples, but must say my first experience has not been fortunate.' All the same, he claimed successfully for damages from the shipping company.

Another old customer, a Mr H. J. Hollins who lived in Southport, wrote asking if Arthur Bell would like to send whisky to South Africa, as he had two friends who had just sailed for Durban and thought they could sell Bell's whisky. Unfortunately there are no records to show whether anything was done in South Africa or

Arthur Bell

not, but Bell wasn't keen on appointing agents he didn't know. After all, he could recruit from his family, as he had done in the past.

For example, he wrote in 1889 to his cousin, Charles Bell, who lived and worked in New Zealand, asking:

if, among your various acquaintances in New Zealand you can recommend any safe and trustworthy house who would have it in their power to introduce my fine old Scottish whiskies in New Zealand. I ship to various parts of the world, but have not yet received any orders from New Zealand. My best old blend of Scottish Whisky is sold here at 8/– per gallon f.o.b. but I have intermediate qualities at 5/–, 6/– and 7/– per gallon.

Being also connected with the firm of Laidlaw and Sandeman, Galashiels, of which firm my nephew Abbott Fitzroy Sandeman is partner along with me, we have some 80,000 gallons of various ages and qualities selected from the best distilleries in Scotland.

My son Arthur has been learning the business with a wholesale firm in Edinburgh for the last three and a half years, and in six months more he will join me here, and I am very anxious to have a good colonial connection, so that he may be independent of the Home Trade, which is so much cut up with keen competition.

The 'keen competition', of course, was from the other whisky firms. There was a real fight on for the home market, though Arthur Bell was apparently worrying more about profits than actual sales. He had given in at last to the idea of appointing agents, though he was still worried about bad debts. He started with an agent in London, then followed Manchester and Leicester, for the towns in the Midlands. The team of agents was made up to six, with two agents in the west coast of England and one in the south.

Bell was pleasantly surprised at the result of these appointments. He wrote to his agent in Southport congratulating him and added, 'There is little doubt that, owing to the demand from England for the finest qualities of Highland whisky, Scotch whisky is rapidly coming into general use across the Border.' This was certainly true, for in the seaside resort of Brighton Bell's were selling more than seven hundred gallons a year.

Arthur Bell now had his eldest son, Arthur Kinmond Bell, in the business. Since the son was known throughout his life as 'A.K.', I shall call him by these initials throughout the rest of this story,

Old casks in Bell's warehouse, Perth

otherwise we might get mixed up between father and son. Mr Bell
put his son on to the touchy job of getting an agent in Australia and
A.K. wrote to his 'ancient mate', Newton Wanliss, who had emi-
grated and was now a solicitor in Ballarat. Wanliss's reply is interesting, because it shows what conditions in the whisky business
were like in Australia at the time.

In his letter Wanliss mentioned he had been unable to fix up an
agent in Ballarat but had got in touch with a friend in Melbourne
who suggested a Mr A. S. Mussabini of that town. In his letter
Wanliss said:

It is not an easy thing to get an agency out here on account of
the expense of advertising, etc., to which the agent is put to
work up the business. The duty on liquor also is severe. In

addition to that, the Temperance party has been very active in late years and I should not be surprised before many years are over Victoria becomes a prohibition colony, i.e. the sale of spirituous liquors being forbidden except in Druggists' shops as medicine.

Wanliss's friend put in an oar in favour of Mr Mussabini. He wrote, 'I can recommend Mr Mussabini as a likely person to make the business hum as he is a man of great energy. He is a gentleman, was educated at Rugby and is engaged to a girl here so will soon settle down into a steady, non-sporting, ratepaying, peaceful citizen.'

He also enclosed A. S. Mussabini's business card which showed that the firm were ship-brokers, general commission agents and indentors in Melbourne and already were sole agents for a wheen of firms, dealing variously with chemicals, tartaric acid, Indian condiments, steel-wire ropes, marine patents, engineers' brass and gun-metal fittings, anti-fouling and soapstone paints, dry and earth colours and dyes, encaustic and art tiles, brushware, lubricating oil, and sheep dip. Taking on a whisky agency with that lot would certainly make life interesting for Mr Mussabini, though one hopes that he would keep the whisky well away from the sheep dip.

Arthur Bell wrote to A. S. Mussabini in Melbourne and proposed certain terms. In his letter agreeing with these terms, Mussabini wrote back assuring Mr Bell that 'although we have done nothing hitherto in wine and spirits, our Mr Mussabini has had ten years' experience in a leading London firm, consequently we anticipate no difficulty in very soon making a start after we get the samples.'

Now it was a question of what blend would suit the market in Australia. Mussabini was inclined for the cheap blends, but Bell wrote to him:

I see by your letter that the great majority of the whiskies sold in Melbourne are 'utter filth, being subordinated to the frantic advertising' and I think that this is the more reason why I should keep up the quality, and only export No. 6, which you could push among merchants, clubs and private gentlemen and, when once tried, would be sure to keep its hold owing to the quality being so superior to what is usually sold in Melbourne.

You might also get orders by explaining to your friends that the reason I can keep up the quality is that I do *not* advertise.

This idea of not advertising had been a bee buzzing in Bell's bonnet for a long time, but he kept a file of letters which he would show to prove that he was right. A man in Sussex, for example, wrote to say, 'I was at the Station Hotel, Perth, a few weeks ago and was so much pleased with the whisky supplied there that I asked who supplied it. They referred me to you. Will you let me know price by case, 2 doz., of same whisky as you supply to Station Hotel.'

A business man in Manchester asked for the price of Bell's whisky because 'I had a present from a friend and like it better than what I have previously bought.' Then there was the Derby chartered accountant who wrote, 'Mr. N. Foley, wine and spirit merchant of Yorkshire Grey, Fitzroy Square, London, whom we met at Blackpool in September last kindly gave us your name as supplying about the best *Old* Scotch Whisky that he could obtain anywhere.' A gentleman living in Enfield wrote to order another case and ended

Arthur Kinmond Bell, 1901

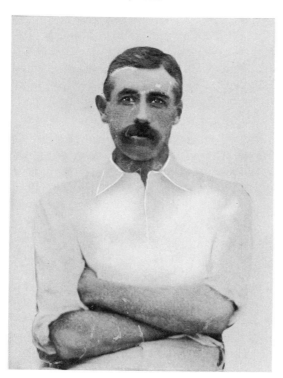

his letter, 'I never met with any whisky to equal it.'

The owner of the Durness Hotel in Sutherlandshire asked for 'Three doz. quarts Ex. Spec. Whisky. It is the only whisky my visitors will take.' A firm in Manchester wrote, 'At the time of ordering the whisky we forgot to mention that we wanted the same quality as that supplied to the Sale Liberal Club, and recommended to us by Mr Street, and we must compliment you on that special quality, which is very good value.' An order from an Edinburgh man ended, 'I prefer your blend to every other.'

A Mr H. A. Farquhar-Spottiswood wrote on crested notepaper from a Hyde Park address, 'I must say your whisky is the best I ever tasted in my life and I have tried a good many brands.' A reverend gentleman wrote from Heywood Rectory in Lancashire ordering 'another two doz. case of the same whisky as the last – *it is excellent*'.

With enconiums like these, it's not surprising that Arthur Bell decided that he didn't really need advertising to help the sales of his superlative whisky.

But Mr Mussabini had his ideas too. He was worried about the anonymous whisky which Arthur Bell was selling. 'We would suggest that you should think over a suitable "Brand" as a reference,' he wrote. 'We have always considered the name "Pall Mall" very suitable out here, as it has never been applied to any line of goods, and though perhaps hardly suggestive of the Home of Distilleries, is such a very distinctive and attractive name. Thus in the leading commercial columns "Sales of Scotch whisky embrace 30 quarters of Bell's 'Pall Mall' Brand" would look very well.'

Possibly stimulated by his son, A.K., Bell weakened enough to say that he was thinking of bringing out a new and even finer whisky called 'White Heather'. But Mussabini's view was that there was not much point in bringing out a new brand if the agent in Melbourne wasn't allowed to advertise the name. Not only that, but he stuck to his Pall Mall idea and wrote:

There are really so many nauseating brands at all the bars in this city [Melbourne] that a really palatable brand with a dis-tinctive name and a good systematic advertising would very soon command the public taste. . . . When we look at the enormous sale of the Galley whisky and then taste it, it is inconceivable to us what constitutes the public taste.

The Watergate, Perth

As regards advertising, we could only hazard the remark that £250 in both Melbourne and Sydney would be absolutely essential at the lowest estimate and, as we have put the celebrated 'Sunlight Soap' on the market here and had the advertisements under our own particular notice, you can realize from this that we are not likely to waste money in this respect.

But Arthur Bell was adamant about advertising and was convinced he was right when Mussabini quoted a note from the secretary of the prestigious Ballarat Club. Mr Mussabini had sent the secretary a sample, and got the reply, 'I think the whisky is superb'. Bell said what he must have thought was his last word on the subject:

You mention that the whiskies which are largely advertised, such as the Galley whisky and others, are utter trash but it stands to reason that no exporter can ship a good quality if he is called upon to expend such large sums in advertising, and I have decided not to advertise, but to try what can be done by the quality alone.

Our advantage, and I may say a good one, is that you will find that when, once tried, your customers will stick by you when they find they are getting a first-class whisky.

At this point, when Arthur Bell was thinking of expanding into Tasmania, Ceylon and New Zealand, he sent his second son, Robert Duff Bell, and his daughter Louie on a holiday to the southern hemisphere to visit the far-flung relations of the Bell and Sandeman families. Robert Bell has been hardly dealt with by those who recall the old days of the growth of the firm. He is supposed to have been something of a playboy, and it is true that, once his elder brother, A.K., took over the firm after their father's death, Robert gradually eased himself out of the responsibilities of helping to run a business that was getting rather beyond him. But undoubtedly he put in a power of work on what was supposed to be his holiday in the spring and summer of 1892.

In Australia Robert and Louie went to Melbourne, and, at his father's request, Robert made contact with the famous Mussabini. His letter from the Grand Hotel, Melbourne, tells a great deal about Mussabini, Melbourne and himself. I have pruned it slightly but, in essence, here it is:

My dear Papa,
Since writing last, which was on Tuesday last, I have found that the Bank made a mistake in saying that the 1 Hogshead, 2 Quarters, 4 Octaves were out of Bond and likely sold. As, when Mussabini returned to town on Saturday last in response to wires I sent him, I asked him if that was the case and he

said no, that none of that lot had been sold but was still in Bond.

Of course, his reason for not paying the Bill was that he could not, only having a very little cash of his own and just keeping afloat and no more, and as he is a very decent fellow to speak to and seemed to feel his position keenly and he told me that if I were to compel him to pay up, it would simply mean his ruin. So, seeing that the whisky was all there, and being sorry for him, I offered to take over the whisky, he handing me over the warrants for same and signing an agreement saying that he pays all expenses, including shipping, cartage, rent, etc., up to date of transferring, all of which I got him to do, but not without some trouble.

Of course he gives up the agency and I am not sorry, as I don't care for his modes of business. He sells the same article at various prices and he also takes in a quarter cask into his office and fills small jars from it and then sells to his friends, which of course (he not holding a licence) might get himself and perhaps your name into trouble, so I was rather glad to get the whisky out of his hands altogether.

As we go to Ballarat for this month I have handed the warrants (seven in all) over to the Bank for safe keeping. I called on Messrs. Jas. Henty & Co. and they asked me to call again today at 11 with samples. As they are the oldest and about the safest firm in town, I will try them on with the agency or, if they won't have it, perhaps they will buy some of the whisky and advise me of some other firm who might take it. I will let you know the result of my call at the end of this letter. Of course it was a great nuisance Mussabini being from home all last week as I could do nothing till I saw him.

Melbourne is in an awfully depressed state just now, lots of people failing. On Sunday last we saw the Earl of Hopetoun's son christened, which was very interesting. We are enjoying ourselves to the full but I leave all news for Louie to give as I am pretty busy today.

The money that is spent here in advertising must be something enormous and they say nothing can be done here without it. We have had some rain here but the weather on the whole has been very good and we have seen all that is to be seen in Melbourne, which is certainly a wonderful town.

I have just called on Messrs Henty but, as it is mail day,

they asked me to call tomorrow, when they would have a long talk with me re the agency. They are *very* nice gentlemen indeed and I will do my best to get them to take on the agency. I do not wish to make any business calls till I get an agent to go round with me and introduce me, so that they won't care about turning me to the door so readily as they would if I went an utter stranger.

With love to all, I remain

Your loving son,

Robert D. Bell.

Robert wrote later to his brother, A.K., from Ballarat. The two sons thought their father was wrong in his attitude to advertising and to brand names, but they hesitated to say so. In this letter to A.K., however, Robert wrote, 'The competition in whisky here is worse than at home and people will have nothing unless a well-known brand – in fact, they are brand mad. Everything is brand, brand, brand. All the fences miles into the bush are plastered over with Claymore Whisky, Robertson's J.R.D. Whisky, Galley Brand Whisky, Buchanan's House of Commons, Dawson's Whisky, etc., etc., too numerous to mention.'

Robert Duff Bell was no fool, even though he was young and out to enjoy himself on what was primarily a holiday. One of his most revealing letters was written from Ballarat on 23 May 1892:

My dear Papa,

Thanks very much for your letter enclosing your copy of Mussa's, your answer to same which I was glad to get. You might also thank dear wee Mabel [his sister] for hers. Tell her it was a perfect treat. She writes such nice homely letters.

Since writing last, which was to Atty [A.K. Bell, his elder brother], the principal news is as follows. On the 19th I called at the Ballarat Club and introduced myself to Mr Barclay, the Secretary, and he appointed me an Honorary Member and then I introduced the subject of business. When Mussa was our agent he quoted the 9/– blend to them at the modest price of 12/6 but they would not have it at the price, so I told Barclay if he would take the whole consignment I could let it go at 10/6, which he jumped at and, as he and several others like the whisky extremely, I think they will buy the above parcel.

George Street, Perth

Robert goes into various price details, always to the benefit of Bell's and says that the secretary of the important Ballarat Club, Mr Barclay,

does not wish to have the transaction [to buy more Bell's whisky] through an agent as he thinks he would get it cheaper through us direct at home. Mussa disposed of an octave at 7/9 nett and I have the money for it. As I thought the above was for a sample cask I let it go, but when I found out he had sold it to Barclay for the Ballater Assembly Balls at 12/- I was wild.

Mussa wired for another at same price, but I gave him to understand he could 'go to pot' first and gave him a lump of my mind at the same time. I have called on several houses here where they were *very pleasant*, but the 9/– blend was too good quality for the trade here.

You would smile if you saw your son bouncing into the office of the Boss and shaking hands and generally giving him a few wrinkles as regards *the trade*, etc., etc. Very funny, I assure you, and I often laugh at myself when I get to the door, and safely out of sight.

Usher has a man here at present kicking up grand rows about the word, or rather Trade Mark, Glenlivet, and making firms take it off their bottles unless it is bought from them, at least so a number of the merchants told me.

But Robert can't stay on business for too long, and he goes on to tell his father of an Australian adventure he has had. And this, I think, tells you more about him than all his animadversions about Mussabini and Melbourne:

I have enjoyed the stay here very much. On last Friday I went a walk of 37 miles!! with a fellow Boyd, brother of Mrs Newton, and another fellow Kennedy. We walked to Learmouth, where we stopped at the village inn and dined with the proprietor, his housekeeper, cook, stable boy and ploughman. It was awful fun and a great fat buxom girl, with her sleeves rolled up to her shoulders, served us and kept rolling her eyes on us whenever any of us spoke.

It was a rummy dinner. You must remember we were right into the back country. It was a regular Bush dinner, consisting of Hare and Rabbit Soup, Boiled Mutton, Stewed Apples and Sago, which only cost us one shilling each. I was only sorry Louie [his sister] wasn't with us! I would like to have seen her sitting next the ploughman and conversing freely with the cook!!

After dinner we walked to Lake Burrunbeet and then home to Ballarat. We left about 8.30 a.m. and walked right on till 7.15 p.m., 1 hour between for dinner. I was pretty stiff next day but felt none the worse of it and the dinner was an experience I would *not* like to have missed.

Today, of course, Robert would have written to his father that he had been 'walkabout'. His letter rambles on in his customary fashion, intermingling business with pleasure and nostalgia about his home in Perth. He ends with a few sharp words about the Australians. 'The people here,' he says, 'are very proud of their country and apt to get a bit cocky, but I don't let them go too far in the way of praise, and if possible they actually try and place it before the old country, which is absurd. You may be sure wherever I am I will always back up good old Scotland.'

Those who regarded Robert Duff Bell as just a hedonist would have been surprised to read the letter he sent his father from Tasmania, where Arthur Bell had asked him to try to find new agents in the North and South regions of the country.

Robert called on Mr Wilmot, of Johnstone and Wilmot of Launceston, Northern Tasmania, and not only sold him whisky on the spot but arranged an agency that fitted in with Arthur Bell's ideas, which wasn't always very easy. He reported to his 'Dear Papa' that Mr Wilmot wanted a case of 'Special Highland Liqueur, as he thought he could find a few customers who liked something "tip-top", as he expressed it'.

And here Robert shows that he did know something about the blending of whisky and the marketing of it as well, because he goes on, 'I know you have not got this blend, but you will remember that, before I left, we thought that some old Glen Grant or Highland Park blended with the 9/- blend would do very well, or another proposal was to get it from R. and B. [Robertson and Baxter] but don't get their Special as it is *far too Islay*.' And he writes in the margin of the letter, 'Of course I had no sample of the Liqueur, so he does not know what it is like!'

The modern methods of blending, packaging and selling used by Bell's today are sophisticated in the extreme, but young Robert Duff Bell had some not bad ideas. 'I think,' he suggested, 'the first plan is the best, viz. blend a quarter cask of the 9/- blend with an octave of 7 or 8 year old Glen Grant, then bottle that off so as to prevent loss in ullage. For the "get up" I would simply label it thus – "Special Highland Liqueur. A. Bell, Perth, N.B." Don't make the colour strong, as a light coloured whisky is liked better out here. Sample the Glen Grant well before blending, as also the 9/- blend, as all future business in Launceston depends on this shipment.'

"Glen Grant" or "Highland Park" blended with the 9/- blend
would do very well or another proposal was
to get it from R.&B. but dont get their Special
as it is far too Islay. I think the first plan
is the best. viz blend a gks cask of the 9/- blend
with an octave of 7 or 8 year old "Glen grant"
(which D & J Robertson would willingly supply)
then bottle that off so as to prevent loss in
ullage. For the "get up" I would simply label
it thus [SPECIAL HIGHLAND LIQUEUR A. BELL PERTH.N.B. / MESS⁵ Johns & Williamt AS INGESTION AGENTS] Liqueur from Perth Scotland
+ tie a their red ribbon round the
outside of case in case of people opening it.
Of course put a capsule on — & dont make the
colour strong as a light-coloured whisky is
liked better out here. Sample the Glen grant
well before blending as also the 9/- blend, as
all future business in Launceston depends on
this shipment. As regards payment Mr Wil
not says you can draw on his bank in London
viz the bank of New South Wales at 60 days sight.
but you can arrange all that with him. They are
a very safe & old established firm & are agents
for Robertsons "J.R.D." whks Dundee as also Mr Hab
Galley Brand, & everyone here speaks highly of
them. I did not mention anything to him about
security as you can well understand how

[left margin, vertical:] Of course I had no sample of the 9/- blend so he does not know what it is like.

Part of the manuscript of Robert Duff Bell's letter,
quoted on the previous page, written to his father
during his Australian trip in 1892

Robert goes on to suggest shipping facilities and then writes rather bashfully, 'I hate making arrangements about money, as I don't understand much about bills, drafts, etc., and I don't care to shew my ignorance to our Agents!!' After all this business talk, he goes on without even starting a new paragraph – 'I am having an awfully jolly time here, shooting every day and playing tennis.'

While young Robert was travelling in Australasia, his brother, Arthur Kinmond Bell, had taken over the blending of Bell's whiskies from their father. Back once again in Melbourne, Robert wrote an admonitory note about his brother Atty's work:

In drawing samples of the shipments [of Bell's whisky] ex 'Gulf of Ancud' and ex 'Lake Superior', the former is much the darker of the two. Atty must be particular in the colouring of these shipments as the people are so suspicious and a difference in the colour is quite enough to make them think they are getting an inferior article. Atty should always keep samples of each shipment and compare same before shipping. The people here are quite ignorant of what composes a good whisky and will only drink something that is fearfully advertised, which game, they say out here, is scarcely worth the candle as the public taste is always changing as regards brands.

Back in Perth, in the year 1895, Arthur Bell made his eldest son, Arthur Kinmond Bell, a junior partner, with one third share of the profits. And he must have been impressed by Robert Duff Bell's work in Australia, New Zealand and Tasmania, for the following year Arthur Bell brought Robert into junior partnership on the same terms as A.K.

The two sons were anxious to expand the business. While they agreed with their father that the quality of Bell's whisky was of paramount importance, they realized that nothing but good could come of advertising a good product. But Arthur Bell could point out to his two new junior partners that the profits of the firm were a mere £1713 in 1890, and now in 1895 were £5726. By that magic year Bell's were exporting their whisky to not only Australia, Tasmania and New Zealand, but also to Ceylon, India, Italy and the South of France.

The other point at issue between father Bell and his sons was the adoption of brand names. Since the time that Arthur Bell had made his sons partners, he gradually faded out of the direct management

D

A group photograph, taken in 1895 outside the still house at Blair Athol. Included are, *centre*, the still house manager, *seated on his left*, the excise officer, *on his right*, the distillery manager, and, *seated far right*, the 'postie'

of the firm and A. K. Bell became the dominant figure. It's a measure of his success that, in the five years between his assumption of junior partnership and the death of his father in 1900, A. K. Bell, with a modicum of help from his brother Robert, had more than doubled the profits of the firm. The £5726 which Arthur Bell boasted of in 1895 had gone up by 1900 to more than £11,000.

One of the last pieces of Victorian wisdom that Arthur Bell passed on to a member of his family, yet another nephew, this time living in Canada, was this: 'If my advice to you is of any use, I would say stick to your Commission or Agency business only, until you have made money to spare to invest in speculative concerns. I think the best motto in business is "slow and sure", but I see the present generation prefer "fast and insecure", and in most cases they land themselves in the *mud*.'

Unfortunately, Elliot Bell in Canada paid little heed to his uncle's good advice and, within a year, was bankrupt.

Arthur Bell died in Perth in the year 1900, leaving a well-founded business to his sons. A.K., the eldest of the family, resolved that he would make Bell's even bigger and better.

A Sticky Wicket

IT's difficult to imagine it in these football-mad days, but at the turn of the century the great game in Perth was cricket. There was a plethora of cricket teams, both official and unofficial. The big team was, of course, Perthshire County Cricket Club and for a number of years their secretary, and later their captain, was Arthur Kinmond Bell. He was still renowned as a cricketer when he virtually took over the family business of Bell's whisky at the age of thirty-one.

A.K., as he was always known, played for his county team but also turned out for the Carlton Club in Edinburgh, opened the innings regularly for Grange, and, when he had reached the ripe age of fifty-five, scored a century for Wolfhill, which may not entitle him to a place in the *Guinness Book of Records* but is a most creditable performance for a middle-aged gentleman.

He was always looking for opportunities to encourage interest in the game and every now and then he would be approached by a group of small boys who wanted to start a cricket team. Invariably he would present them with bats, a ball and cricket stumps and his blessing. It was said of him that he had done more for cricket in Perthshire than any man of his day.

So it could be said that he was the forerunner of the policy of Bell's today, which is to encourage sport in all its forms. And it's interesting that the chairman and managing director today is a sportsman too.

Not that A. K. Bell was the managing director in 1900. He and his brother Robin ran the firm, along with Sandy Thompson, who was a salesman of Bell's whisky by day and secretary by night! In other words, he took his secretarial work home with him because

The Perthshire cricket team, 1909
Standing, umpire; J. Mailer; professional, W. E.
Gregson; H. J. Fraser; R. W. Smith; J. A. Ferguson;
A. Fraser; club secretary, A. Latto; umpire
Seated, R. Gardner; F. Smith; Captain, A. K. Bell;
W. Lovat Fraser; J. Anderson

he was too busy to attend to it during the day.

Arthur Bell, who had built up the firm over many years, was, as
we have seen, a cautious and canny man. But he did lay the right
foundations because of his insistence that quality of the product
should come first. On the other hand, he mistrusted advertising and
had what almost amounted to a phobia about bad debts.

It was time for young ideas to take over and A.K. started a new
era of expansion – perhaps modest judged by the way things go
today, but a good step forward in the late Victorian world of Bell's.
Right away he sent his brother back on a selling trip to Australia
and New Zealand, while he concentrated on expanding the trade
in England.

Gradually the sons had persuaded their father that brand names
on whisky helped to sell the product. Examples of the first labels
still exist and they are remarkable for the fact that the name of

Bell does not appear on them. As far back as 1897 Bell's registered a lable for 'Scotch Fir' Old Scotch Whisky. This shows a Scottish country view which includes a winding river and road, mountains in the background, but not a single fir tree! There is a design of thistles down one side, but nothing to substantiate the name of the whisky.

This was followed, for some reason for which no explanation exists, by the registration of a label for the 'Colleen Brand' of Special Irish. This depicted a sonsy Irish lass, in red cloak and green dress, carrying a basket of eggs. Presumably Bell's were importing Irish whiskey along with the brandies and wines they still dealt with in those days.

These two labels were registered in Arthur Bell's time. When A.K. took over, the style did not change much at first. There's a label for 'Skerryvore' Old Scotch Whisky, showing a moonlight view of a lighthouse, rocks and sea. It's not until 1904 that the name of Bell appears on a registered label. This was famous in its day and was known as the 'Curler' label. It shows a curler in the kilt preparing to throw a stone on the ice and the wording is 'Arthur Bell and Sons Extra Special Old Scotch Whisky, Perth, N.B., established 1825'.

Incidentally, in case any perfervid Scots object to that 'N.B.', it should be explained that it did not mean North Britain, as is generally supposed. The letters stood for North Box, which was a term used by the Post Office in London to expedite the delivery of mail to Scotland.

However, by 1910 Scotland got its proper place on a Bell's label, when the 'Golfer' label was produced. This showed a golfer in somewhat attenuated plus-fours – they might be described as plus-twos in fact – driving from the tee. This time the superscription runs, 'Arthur Bell and Sons Old Scotch Whisky, Perth, Scotland', and the date of the establishment is given.

In 1908 A. K. Bell decided he should pay a selling trip abroad and went to Canada. He had already moved the firm from their original premises to a fine new building in Victoria Street, which was destined to be Bell's headquarters for many years. It is no longer used, but it still stands in the middle of Perth, a rather strange, rabbit-warren of a building but still held in great affection by many of those who worked there.

A.K. concentrated on Canada for some time and a list giving

'Description of customers, made out for future reference by Mr A. K. Bell' shows something of the painstaking way he went about his business. The names of two Montreal men are mentioned and the note goes on, 'Jackson's brother could influence business with the Canadian Pacific Railway Co., while Johnston's wife is a friend of Mr Reid of Newfoundland'. For a firm in Winnipeg he admonishes, 'Labels to be more carefully put on'.

Psychology comes in too. Of the Partners of a business in Portage La Prairie, A.K. writes, 'McCave not communicative. Campbell more sociable. He is to endeavour to get our whisky going in this town. They are thoroughly pleased with our bulk whisky and will probably buy more in future.' Then there's the Gold Coin Liquor Store in Moosejaw. 'Owned by two young fellows. Both keen on business and are to endeavour to push our whisky in Moosejaw.' And of a business in Regina, he says cryptically, 'Office apparently run rather slackly. No one really at head of affairs. The Traveller belongs to Leith. One of the men in store comes from Dundee.'

Old Arthur Bell might well have worried about advertising once again if he had read his son's words on a firm in Vancouver. 'They are building a new store on which we have a painted advertisement. They also wish us to put up an electric sign on top of new building, which will be seen all over Vancouver Harbour.' Of a licence holder in Nelson, he writes, 'Good Scotchman. Too careful.' And of one in Fernie, 'Good, sociable man. Coming to Scotland. Business in district spoiled by Coal Strike. Sells principally cheap qualities.'

But whether or not Mr Fernie ever got to Scotland is doubtful, for not long after these notes were written the Great War of 1914–18 broke out. Most of the young men on Bell's staff joined up. For the first time women were employed by the firm. The price of whisky rose. When, eventually, it reached 12s. 6d. a bottle, A. K. Bell was observed to shake his head sadly and say, 'This is the end of our business!'

Two young girls joined the office staff in the last year of the war. They were Jenny and Georgina Hill. They are still living in Perth and attended Bell's 150th anniversary dinner in Glasgow in 1975. The elder sister, Jenny, was the first to enter Bell's service. An extra girl was needed for a week so she suggested she should bring in her sister Georgina. The following Monday Georgina returned to the office and settled down to work as usual. Nobody told her to go and she stayed in the job for thirty-eight years! That, at any rate, is the story told at Bell's to this day.

The Misses Hill retired some years ago and live in one of the pleasant cottages on the Gannochy Housing Estate, built by A. K. Bell in the twenties. They are full of life and fun and they have very fond memories of A.K., whom they regarded as a paragon of all the virtues.

'He was always so polite and considerate,' they say, and, as an example, tell gleefully the story of the very small and rather immature office boy who was coming back from his lunch-hour to the office in Victoria Street when he spied on the way the imposing figure of his boss, A. K. Bell. Quite happily the office boy crossed the street and fell into step with Mr Bell, who did not seem in the least perturbed by being hailed by the most junior member of the staff. The two of them walked back to the office together, conversing amiably all the way.

The war ended on 11 November 1918, and business gradually came back to normal. As in the days of his father, A. K. Bell still had the Bank of Scotland as the firm's bankers. From the Edinburgh headquarters of the Bank I got the note, 'From 1901 until November, 1920, the account was conducted on regular lines with occasional disagreement between the firm and the Bank regarding the rate of discount of Bills.' History keeps repeating itself, as we know, and to this day there are the occasional disagreements on discount rates between Bell's and the Bank of Scotland. Both businesses seem to keep flourishing, however!

In December, 1921, the partnership of Arthur Bell and Sons was made into a limited company with a capital of £350,000. A. K. Bell became what was called 'governing director' of the firm. His brother Robin was by now little more than a sleeping partner.

But although the business was expanding, there was still a family feeling in the firm. This is nicely put over in a piece of homespun verse by one, Joe Chalmers, a Bell's employee. The poet himself read it at the 100th anniversary dinner given to the male members of the staff by A.K., and it was considered so good that copies of the effusion were printed and still exist. It's worth reproducing in full because it gives a close description of some of the people in the firm and what they did. Although it's a very good-natured affair, it's called 'Some Home Truths'.

One of Bell's first labels, issued in 1897 for 'Scotch
Fir' Old Scotch Whisky

Label for 'Skerryvore' Scotch whisky, issued about
1901–2

The famous 'Curler' label, issued in 1904 and the first
to actually show Bell's name

The 'Golfer' label, issued in 1910

It runs :

> I'll start wi' our host, Mr Bell,
> For he always does us well:
> Be it wages, work or pleasure
> He deals it oot in richt guid measure.
>
> And Mr Robin's he's no able
> Tae join us at oor festive table:
> I am sorry for that too,
> We dinna see much o' him noo.
> But he minds us a' the same
> When he sends us doon some game,
> A pair o' rabbits or a hare
> Keeps the cupboard frae bein' bare.
> I ken that I am no alane
> When I thank him for that same.
>
> There is Mr Thompson tae,
> He has a lot o' wark tae dae –
> 'Tween workers and the office staff
> He hasna much time tae pit aff.
> But he does it wi' precision:
> A worthy man in his position.
>
> There is Mr Donald Mackay,
> Tae speak o' him I'm kind o' shy.
> You see, as yet, we've never met,
> We hope tae ken him better yet.
>
> And Mr Ince I see there too,
> A member o' the Revenue,
> His wark is tae collect the Duty
> What the Government claim for their booty.
> We'll maybe hear him later on
> On his mouth-organ gramophone.
>
> Then Forbes, in warehouse duty-paid,
> There for himself a place has made,
> And I havena ony doobt
> That he kens what he's aboot.

And, of course, there's Jimmie Clark
Richt up tae his ears in wark,
But with me you will agree
He does well in the Duty free.

This while back we've been sae busy
It wad nearly mak' ye dizzy.
It taks muscle, aye, and brain
Just to keep the hale thing gain'.
My shirt is often wringin' wet:
What's that ye say? Of course it's sweat.
There's Willie Welsh oot at the double,
He's the cause o' a' the trouble,
Look at the orders that he's bringin'
Just tae keep the Bell's aye ringin'.

And Mr Ferguson ower there,
I know contributes his share,
And Dan Crichton by the way
Did the same thing in his day.
Maybe noo he's no' sae frisky,
Still he likes his gless o' whisky.

Dunc. MacLean looks gie queer
When he's six or seven casks tae clear.
He puts oot mair wark in a day
Than we can across the way.
But he needna think we're dottled,
There's a lot tae dae afore it's bottled.

I see that Geordie Fyffe is laughin',
He can stand a lot o' chaffin'.
Geordie, what hae ye been daein',
Ye're gettin thin I've heard ye sayin'?
Let's hae a look at ye my laddie,
Ye'll shin be wasted tae a shaddie.

Then up comes the filling book,
Harry goes and has a look,
There's six or seven pages there,
It's then Harry starts tae swear.

They'll no get a' that stuff the nicht
But Harry manages it a' richt.
He starts wi' energy tae pack,
There's seldom anything kept back.

If you want a job done quick,
Inglis there will dae the trick,
For rushin' it Jack has a thirst
He will dae the job or burst.

Then Bob Fyall and Geordie Broon
Tak' the stuff oot roond the toon,
Noo-a-days they get a larry,
Auld Tam had tae use a barry.

Morrison comes in and asks,
Sandy, are ye needin' casks?
Irvine says I dinna ken,
Ye'd better maybe bring in ten.

Honeyman goes thro' his paces,
Tryin' tae keep us gaun wi' cases.

Just wait a wee, I've some mair yet,
The lassies we canna forget,
It's a pity they werena here,
Just tae join us in oor cheer,
But of coorse that wadna dae,
For we couldna hae oor say.

There is no a day that passes
But we're gled tae hae the lassies,
I ken that they are feelin' hit
Because tonight they're out of it.

Noo this rigmarole is ended
I hope there's nane of ye offended.
When there's wark tae dae it's done wi' zest,
I ken that we a' try oor best.

As I say, this 'rigmarole' is interesting because of the light it
sheds upon Bell's in the early twenties. Compared with today, the
operation was a very small one. One horse-drawn lorry was all that

A horse-drawn lorry at Glasgow docks

was needed for local deliveries of whisky. In that year of 1922 the net profits were £43,431 17s. 8d. Advertising had reached the dizzy heights of £479 12s. 10d, a figure which would have horrified Arthur Bell.

That year was also interesting for two very different reasons. First, because A. K. Bell bought the farms and lands of Gannochy and Muirhall in the Parish of Kinnoull for £18,400, and that marks the origin of the Gannochy Trust, through which Bell's have given so much to the City of Perth. Second, because 1920 was the year in which the United States of America adopted Prohibition and went 'dry' – officially, at least!

There was an immediate slump in the whisky trade and it seemed to affect Bell's, even though their exports to America were negligible. And, although A.K. announced at the annual general meeting of the company in May, 1924, that Bell's export trade was improving, especially in New Zealand, he also had to announce that the profit for the year 1923 was £23,295 18s. 4d., little more than half the profit

Throwing away wines and spirits in Boston during the
height of Prohibition, 1920

of 1922. On the other hand, advertising had cost over £1000. Meanwhile Gannochy and good works were much in his mind. The new
cottages had started to go up at Gannochy, and Bell's also bought
Kincarrathie House with its extensive grounds. And, although the
profits were down, the firm also bought a sawmill in Victoria Street
adjacent to the offices and used it to expand their operations.

A 'new boy' attending that annual general meeting in 1927 was
a young chartered accountant named William Govan Farquharson,
who was destined to become an important figure in the development of Bell's. At the beginning of the Great War he had gone
straight from school into the Royal Scots, known as 'Pontius
Pilate's Bodyguard' because they were the oldest regiment in the
British Army. He was a vigorous young man and won the Battalion
Boxing Championship as a middle-weight. By the end of the war
he was Captain W. G. Farquharson, M.C. Then, when he was de-

mobilized, he became an apprentice C.A. He was very glad to get a job on the staff of Bell's because jobs were scarce and ex-soldiers were wondering what had happened to the promised 'Land fit for heroes to live in'.

Today, when the fashion is to admire the Roaring Twenties, people are apt to forget that that decade was not all 'Bright Young Things', flappers in short skirts, Bertie Woosters in Oxford bags, and dancing the Charleston at tea-time. As far as Bell's were concerned, the state of trade in the country was shown by another big drop in profits. For 1924 the profit was down to £11,281 18s. 9d. But A.K. was not disheartened. He announced that the firm had bought one of the largest bonded warehouses in Leith and said, 'This will afford convenient facilities which are likely to be required in the future for handling the Export Trade.'

This warehouse was at Whitfield Lane, 117 Leith Walk, and was a very substantial building indeed. It was six storeys in height and was known locally as Ainslie's No. 1 Excise Bond. In the twenties it was considered an ideal place for the bonding and bottling of

The building in Victoria Street, Perth, to which Bell's moved in 1908, and which remained their headquarters for many years

The bonded warehouse in Leith acquired by Bell's
in 1924

whisky. Today it would be regarded as something like a prison,
with its barred windows and very limited facilities. But the description furnished by Ainslie, Baillie and Co. Ltd (In Voluntary
Liquidation) to A. K. Bell makes it seem the perfect building to
acquire.

I will quote only one of the building's attractions that were
offered. 'There is,' said the Ainslie report to Bell's, 'in the Bottling
Cellar a Rotary Pump, Patent Filter, Bottling Filling Machine,
Labelling Machine and Nailing Machine, all worked with electric
motor, besides other machines. The bottling capacity is about 400
dozen per day.'

This, in the light of Bell's production at that time, was very
attractive to A.K. It meant that Leith could produce about

125,000 cases of whisky a year, which to him was a very fine feat indeed. He could never have envisaged that the time would come when his firm would produce more than 3,000,000 cases in a year.

Like his father, A.K. was a compulsive letter writer to the newspapers. While his main interest was the production of Bell's whisky, he was also bound up in housing, cricket, good works and the general improvement of his native city. Most of his letters went to the *Perthshire Advertiser*, and I have picked one of them, not only because it shows his excellent epistolary style, but because it put forward an idea that he altered completely in his later days.

It appeared in the *Perthshire Advertiser* for 5 November 1924, and it read:

Sir, – Is it not being taken too much for granted that the proposed Loch Ordie Water Scheme must be proceeded with?

A supply of water from the hills by gravitation is doubtless the best scheme for a city to adopt. Circumstances, however, have to be considered, and when one of our Councillors advises us to proceed with the Ordie scheme 'no matter what the cost', we hesitate and ask – Is this wise counsel, and if it is not possible to overestimate the benefits?

In years gone by the inhabitants of our Fair City have been reared on the water from the Tay, and there would be no water question today had we not continued, when our numbers increased, to pour our sewage into it. Is there any town the size of Perth that discharges its sewage directly into the river, at its door, and is there no likelihood that sooner or later we will have to conform to more modern methods?

Considering the foregoing, is it not a matter of sewage we have to deal with, and could the water question, as well as that of the sewage, not be settled by one operation, and at very much less expense, viz. by means of settling ponds or by taking the sewage down the river to a point from which it would be impossible to reach our filter beds with the incoming tide?

The Council appears to me to be about to put the cart before the horse, and will certainly be doing so if, after spending £300,000 or more on a gravitation scheme, we are told to go and purify our river.

I am, etc.,
A. K. Bell.

E

"I WANT TO BE HAPPY": JIMMY (MR. JOSEPH COYNE), BILLY (MR. GEORGE GROSSMITH), WITH THE MISSES JOAN BARRY, VERA PEARCE, AND FLORENCE BAYFIELD.

The finale of the number 'I want to be happy' from the show *No No Nanette*

If A.K. was wrong in this, he was certainly right in his prognostication that it was worth buying the bonded warehouse in Leith because of likely increases in Bell's export trade. In the spring of 1926 he was able to announce a profit which was nearly trebled from the previous year. The 1925 result was £29,161 5s. 9d. as against 1924's £11,000. The Leith warehouse was being fitted up for another increase in trade and the export business, in his terms, was booming.

The year of 1925 was also a happy one for Bell's because they celebrated their centenary. The celebrations, compared with those of the 150th year, were modest, but Bell's was a modest firm in 1924 if you measure it by the position of Bell's today.

There were various celebration parties and, as you'll have observed from 'Some Home Truths', there was still a separation of the sexes. The men on Bell's staff had a dinner in the Victoria Hotel in Perth, but the women had a special celebration of their own. A. K. Bell sent them to a performance of the most famous musical comedy of the twenties, *No No Nanette!* which had its British première at the Alhambra Theatre in Glasgow. This show had received the accolade of approval of the Prince of Wales, the darling of Britain who later reigned briefly as King Edward VIII and became the Duke of Windsor when he abdicated. He had seen *No No Nanette!* in New York and came back with records of the two most popular numbers from the show, 'Tea for Two' and 'I Want to be Happy'.

The centenary was a happy affair, and A.K. had another reason for happiness. He was absorbed in the Gannochy Housing Estate, which he had started with the idea of supplying cheaply-rented houses for Perth railwaymen who had been laid off work. In the course of time, other deserving people in Perth occupied the houses too, and A.K. was delighted in 1925 that the Gannochy Housing Estate was now in being and a number of Perth people were already living there (see plate IV).

As the Gannochy cottages were increasingly occupied, A.K. developed the habit of walking round the housing estate early every morning before he went into the office in Victoria Street. His object was to see that everything about the estate was in good shape – and also that the inhabitants were keeping the windows open! A.K. was a very healthy man himself and a great walker, and he believed that the way to stay healthy was to sleep with the windows open. He even had special posters prepared, which were distributed among the Gannochy tenants, explaining how important an open window was and that, if you felt the cold, all you had to do was to put another blanket on your bed.

If, on his morning perambulation, he discovered a house with all the windows closed, he would call on the occupiers then and there, and deliver a little lecture, more in sorrow than in anger, on the importance of open windows.

But his outside interests, in which the game of cricket still bulked largely, did not interfere with his preoccupation with the blending and selling of whisky. He had said optimistic words about the export trade but he was worried enough about business in England to ask a certain H. Nelson James, who was a renowned traveller for one of the brandies which Bell's sold, to investigate the provincial English market for him. Mr James sent a long letter to A.K. after he had investigated seventeen firms. He wrote of these firms, 'Some of them are small, but as your whisky is at present unknown in some of these towns, it would be as well to open out with as many as possible, as when your quality is known, good business is bound to follow.'

Perhaps his most important mention was that of the firm of H. D. Scott, 99 High Street, Ventnor, Isle of Wight. It read, 'Just the man for you in the Island. Also does a nice private trade with good class people in England. Is well in with the Royal Yacht Squadron, Cowes.'

But you could work very hard in the whisky business and still be affected by matters outwith your control. In 1926 the profit fell from £29,000 to £17,000 'owing to excessive duty on spirits'. By 1927 it had gone up like a yo-yo to £25,000. In 1928, when advertising was now costing £11,000, it was up to nearly £27,000. The upward trend continued in 1929, even though the Australian Government raised the tariff wall so as to practically exclude Scotch whisky from their country. Next year there was a dramatic fall from nearly £25,000 to £14,000, and in 1931 the profit plummeted to a mere £4000.

This fall was not confined to Bell's. A.K. said, 'Owing to the continuance of the present exorbitant duty on whisky, together with the world-wide depression, both our Home and Export trade have still further declined. But as far as the company's lower sales are concerned, the decrease is probably not nearly so great in proportion as the decrease in the Scotch Whisky Trade as a whole.'

But worse was to come. For 1932, for the first time in their history, Bell's had to declare a loss. The sum was £10,952 7s. 1d. 'The consumption of Scotch whisky continues to fall,' said A.K. 'Even more serious is the alarming fall in the value of wood. Your directors have decided to write down the value of the company's casks and the casks now stand at market prices. Although this is only wise, it unfortunately means, even after your Managing Director has decided to forgo his interest on his loan and his fee as Director, that the profits that would have been available to pay a dividend on the ordinary shares have been wiped out.'

A. K. Bell must have thought of his father's hard times, when

Arthur Bell decided to take no money from the business so that it would stay on an even keel.

All was not doom and despair, however, in that traumatic year of 1932. Whatever was happening to the whisky business, all was going well with the Gannochy Housing Estate. The building of the estate had attracted great attention over the years and many important visitors had been shown round it. Now the last house, for the time being, had been completed and the architects and contractors decided to make a presentation to A.K.

A.K. and his wife invited them to supper first of all at his home, Kincarrathie House in Perth (see plate III). And so, on an evening in April, the presentation took place. R. M. Mitchell, F.R.I.B.A., one of the architects, made the presentation and in the course of his speech said,

After seven years of steady work the Gannochy Housing Scheme of Messrs Arthur Bell and Sons, Ltd, has been completed. With its completion a spontaneous and unanimous feeling was expressed amongst those who have had the privilege and pleasure of being associated with you in the carrying out of this splendid piece of work that the occasion must not be allowed to pass without special notice.

The scheme that has been carried out is of a most extensive and comprehensive character, and one that has met with the unqualified approval of the many housing experts who have examined it. Perhaps I might be permitted to recall what Mr Neville Chamberlain, the Chancellor of the Exchequer, said when shown over the site, while the scheme was progressing. He said, 'I have visited many housing schemes, but this one is unique in character and certainly the best I have seen.'

Sir John Gilmour, the then Secretary of State for Scotland, also expressed himself in almost simular terms of approval.

The material and workmanship throughout are of the highest class and, besides providing a large measure of much needed employment in the community, the scheme has served the double purpose of affording a fine opportunity for many young men to learn their respective trades. The houses themselves have met a sorely felt want, because they have provided the latest and most modern accommodation for a section of the community for which no adequate provision has been made in

The cricket field and Pavilion, Doo'cot Park

the city. The business relations among clients, contractors and architects have been of the happiest description, and every man who was on the job has the most pleasing memories of your personal consideration and courtesy at all times.

Sir, will you permit us to mark the event by the presentation to you of a small remembrance of your firm's magnificent contribution of 150 houses towards the solution of the housing problem in Scotland. The picture is a memento of our long and happy association and with it we wish to convey to you our sincere esteem and our indebtedness for your unfailing and generous kindness to every one of us.

We congratulate you most warmly on the completion of your firm's large hearted and deeply appreciated housing scheme and on the successful realization of the fine ideal to which you personally have so faithfully adhered in the years that have gone.

Amid applause Mr Mitchell presented A.K. with a large water colour painting showing an aerial view of the Gannochy housing estate by the distinguished architectural artist, Cyril Farey. You can still see it today if you visit the building in the grounds of Kincarrathie House in which the Board of Directors of Bell's used to meet.

After the presentation A.K. replied and then there were more speeches, and special mention was made of the fine cricket field and pavilion which A. K. Bell had provided at Doo'cot Park, next to Kincarrathie House. The cricket ground and pavilion are still very much in use to this day and some notable games of cricket have been played there.

In 1932, of course, A.K. was President of the Perthshire Cricket Club, and had also been elected President of the Grange Cricket Club in its centenary year.

I can't leave this pleasant scene of the dinner at Kincarrathie House without mentioning one point which came up in post-prandial discussion. It had nothing to do with cricket or with whisky, but it's perhaps a tribute to the buirdly men of Perth, who have a reputation for knowing their whisky. It turned out that the ages of two of the contractors who had worked on the Gannochy housing estate, David Taylor and John Brown, reached 'the magnificent total of 172 years, and it was an inspiring sight to note the splendid vigour of body and character so evident in them both'.

So, after all, 1932 wasn't such a bad year, despite the loss that Bell's had sustained. And better times were just around the corner.

The Way to War

THE UNITED STATES OF AMERICA repealed their Prohibition laws in 1933, and the sun started to shine on the whisky makers once again. Things didn't change overnight, of course, but there was a steady improvement. The worst of the world recession seemed to be over too, and the only disappointed people were the pessimists who had been sure that, this time, the civilized world was finished.

As far as Arthur Bell and Sons, Ltd, were concerned, it was a courageous time of expansion. They had bought a bonded ware-house at Auchtermuchty 'on reasonable terms', and now they set out to acquire the well-established Edinburgh firm of P. Mackenzie and Co., Distillers Ltd, who owned two good Highland malt distilleries, the Blair Athol Distillery at Pitlochry (which had actually been established one year after Bell's started), and the Dufftown-Glenlivet Distillery at Dufftown, sometimes called the 'Golden City' because so much fine malt whisky is made and stored there. Blair Athol had actually been closed down by Mackenzie because of the slump, and Dufftown-Glenlivet was just ticking over.

The price paid by Bell's to Mackenzie for the business was £56,000 and it was well worth it. In Dufftown, Pitlochry and Edinburgh the Mackenzie firm had stored in warehouses over 120,000 proof gallons of Highland, Islay, Campbeltown and Lowland malt whiskies, together with some grain whiskies and whisky already blended. But what was important was that nearly 80 000 of these proof gallons were excellent Highland malt whiskies.

A. K. Bell negotiated the buying himself, and dealt with a Mr H. S. Dove, who was managing director of Mackenzie's and lived

in style at St Boswells in the Borders. The take-over was conducted
on the most friendly terms and Mr Dove was apt to add such a
chatty comment to his letter as, 'Please excuse typing as I have
just returned after a very long Otter Hunt.'

Another bonus for Bell's was that the firm of P. Mackenzie had
been established in the American market before Prohibition came
in and still retained their connections in the United States. Mr Dove
wrote to A.K.:

It may interest you to know that a letter has just come to
hand at this moment from one of our American agents, who
says that it is their immediate intention to shortly cable
substantial orders for warehousing in the U.S. Government
Bonded Warehouses, and others which they desire us to hold
and for which they will pay for immediately. They say that
they will probably order 10 to 12 thousand cases. This looks
cheerful.

Cheerful was the word. In his annual report for 1933 A.K. was
able to announce that distilling had started once more at Dufftown-
Glenlivet and that the quality of the new make was excellent. But
that was just an appetizer. He went on to reveal that the loss of
£10952 of 1932 had been transformed into a profit of £28,432 in
1933.

For W. G. Farquharson 1933 was a very important year. He was
invited to join the board of directors, and A. K. Bell sent him out
on a selling and investigative trip which included Australia, New
Zealand, Egypt and India. Obviously A.K. liked the young man.
He wrote to Bell's agents in Wellington, New Zealand, 'Mr
Farquharson is now well on his way, and should be at Bombay
today. His letters are most interesting. He is very keen on his job
and looks forward to his New Zealand visit.'

And to W. G. Farquharson himself, A.K. wrote a private and
personal note. It is a very revealing one.

Dear Mr Farquharson [wrote A.K.], I called at your home
last night and saw Mrs Farquharson who showed me your
snapshots. I am glad to say your wife is well and your young-
sters, who were running all over the place, did not seem to be
missing you.

Glad to see you are fit. Well, I hope you will *keep fit* and not
drink too much of that stuff – Bells. New Zealand is more

Bell's advertising in New Zealand in the 1930s

dangerous than Australia. Don't try and keep up with Reid and tell Barry's man to go to H—l. Moffett also goes too strong.

My point is, do not spoil your health for the sake of business. I nearly did so the *first* time I was out.

Yours sincerely,
A. K. Bell.

A.K.'s warning about New Zealand having its social dangers is backed up every now and then by letters sent to Farquie (as he was familiarly called). Cyril A. Hughes, one of the partners of an Auckland importing firm, wrote to him at Wellington saying that he had sent a Bell's bottle to an important agent in Sydney, Australia, and added, 'The Chamber of Commerce Ball takes place on Thursday evening and, as we told you, we are exhibiting Bell's Whisky, having a Scotchman in his uniform, and a lady also dressed in a suitable uniform, to represent this whisky. We are only sorry that you are not here to attend this function.'

Mr Hughes' letter to Sydney said in part:

Mr W. G. Farquharson, director of Messrs Arthur Bell & Sons,
Ltd, Perth, Scotland, has requested us to forward you a package
containing an OVAL BOTTLE, with a Cork which can be
opened by hand, and an Aluminium Drinking Cup on the top.
Mr. Farquharson requests us to ask you if this would not be a
very suitable type of package for you to import, more especially
for the Trade in the Bottle Stores of Hotels throughout New
South Wales.

We might say that we are Agents in the Auckland Province
of New Zealand for Bell's, and one outstanding feature in regard
to the sale of their Whisky is that it is packed in clear Bottles,
and it is very difficult to add Water, on account of the Bottle
being clear. When water is added, after a few days the Whisky
generally becomes cloudy.

After recommending the Oval Bottle in the Carton, Mr Hughes
adds that its advantage is that 'it can be carried away in a disguised
form'. And of miniature bottles of Bell's whisky he says, 'These
small Bottles are sold in the Bottle Stores here at 1/6 each. There
is very little profit in them, but they are a very good Advertising
medium. For instance, in New Zealand the Hotels close at 6 o'clock,
and people will buy these small bottles, conceal them in their
pockets, and if they are going to the Pictures or a Cabaret, the
contents of the bottle are easily consumed and never noticed.'

Mr Hughes finishes with a P.S. 'There is only one regret, that is
that the sample Bottle we are sending is Empty, but the contents
were so good that we drank same. We hope in the future to have the
pleasure of one of your firm visiting us and having a spot "Afore
Ye Go".'

'Afore Ye Go', of course, had already become a slogan for Bell's
whisky, and a very popular one.

Back home A. K. Bell was intrigued to get a letter from J. C. W.
de Haas of Rotterdam:

I beg to inform you [wrote Mr de Haas], that I have the
intention to leave in the course of August next for Manchuria
with residence Harbin. As far as I know, you are not represented
in Manchuria, and I therefore ask you to kindly let me know
whether you should be willing to give me the Agency for your
whisky in Manchuria.

There is a big consumption of Whisky in that country, and
in my opinion it will be possible to do a nice business for you
in future as soon as the consumers will have been convinced of
the first-class quality of your brand. In Manchuria as well as in
the other part of China I am well-introduced having resided and
travelled there some years.

A.K. never missed a trick. He wrote back to Mijnheer de Haas
saying:

We are quite willing that you should have the Agency for our
Scotch Whisky in Manchuria.
The price of our bottled Whisky is: – 42/6 per case of 1 dozen
quarts f.o.b. any port in this Country. Cash against documents
in London.
We could allow you 5/– per case to cover commission and all
your expenses. The only condition we lay down is that we have
power – whether we use it or not – to cancel this Agency should
the shipments to Manchuria be less than 500 cases during any
twelve consecutive months after one year from this date.
If you could do business in China we are open to consider
any proposal, as we are not represented in that country.

Alas, J. C. W. de Haas of Rotterdam does not seem to have come
up to specification. I can't find any trace of business between Perth
and Manchuria in the thirties, far less China. A list of Bell's agents
brought out about that time is impressive. It includes six agents in
Australia and ten in New Zealand. There are other agents in
Ontario, Montreal, New York, Mexico City, Lima, Calcutta,
Colombo, Bangkok, Alexandria, Cairo, Port Said, Kenya, Rhodesia,
Natal, New Guinea, Fiji, Copenhagen, Arnhem, Oslo and Zürich,
but no mention of Manchuria. This, by the way, is a small list
compared with Bell's export trade today, but it was quite an
achievement for the firm in the thirties.
Bell's had, naturally, thoroughly investigated the American
market after the repeal of Prohibition in the United States. They
received a report on the situation from an advertising agency in
New York and it was not exactly encouraging. This report was
made one year after repeal and it said:

It is well known that conditions in the liquor industry since
Repeal have been in a chaotic state, but it is generally believed

that considerable improvement will have been made by early
Fall.

Considering the speed with which Repeal laws were enacted
by the various states, it is not surprising that confusion
developed. The anticipated boom has not materialized.

The advertising agency estimated that there were something like
20,000 brands of liquor on the American market, which included
all kinds of potables besides Scotch whisky. There was also the
fact that, over the years of Prohibition, dreadful products like
'bath-tub gin' were all that was available. Many young and even
middle-aged people had never tasted a matured drink like Scotch
whisky. They were used to raw spirits or strange mixtures and were
called 'The Bootleg Generation'.

The report pointed out that 'Competition does not lie between

Bell's advertising in New York, in the 1930s

Scotch, American and Canadian whiskies, but rather among all types of liquors. To this group, whisky is whisky and a taste for certain kinds or brands is yet to be developed. An investigation in New York showed that the preference for whisky was Rye first of all, Scotch second, and Bourbon third.

Bell's moved rather cannily into the American market. A.K. undoubtedly considered himself a good business man and W. G. Farquharson was a thruster, but habit and conditions were against any big move in the selling of whisky. A.K. was happy that the new acquisition, the Dufftown-Glenlivet Distillery, had had a successful season in 1934, 'the quality being specially remarked upon'. Profits were inclined to move up and down, but for the year 1935 they had reached over £30,000. In the following year A.K. heard that the Inchgower Highland Malt Distillery at Buckie was on the market. The original owner had sold it to Buckie Town Council for £1000 and it was considered a municipal asset for a while. Then, for various reasons, Buckie Town Council decided they didn't want to keep the distillery.

A.K. travelled up to the fishing town on the north-east coast. He saw over the distillery and liked what he saw. He met the Provost of Buckie and they talked money. Eventually, A.K. offered the Provost £3000 for Inchgower and, on behalf of Buckie Town Council, the Provost accepted. As they left the distillery the Provost pointed out to A.K. the mansion house near by which belonged to the distillery. He said it was for sale too. A.K. said, 'I'll give you £1000 for it.' Apparently dazed by this sudden offer, the Provost accepted. In later years he was heard to remark about the occasion, 'It was the first time I was done twice in one day!'

Inchgower is a very pleasant distillery indeed, and I shall be saying more about it later. But I should say at this point that the good folk of Buckie still regard it as a local possession. The whisky that is made at Inchgower is considered to be Buckie whisky and nothing to do with Bell's at all!

Doubtless A.K. was very pleased with the acquisition of Inch-gower Distillery, but the next thing that concerned him was the threat to the linen industry in Perth. It had at one time been a very big industry indeed, but it had declined to just one firm, John Shields and Co., Ltd. In 1936 it was hit by depression and was in danger of closing. A.K. investigated and decided to save the linen industry by buying the business. He became chairman and reorganized and re-equipped the factory. There still exists a parchment in which the senior members and the foremen of the Wallace Works of John Shields record their indebtedness and gratitude to Arthur Kinmond Bell.

That same year that he received the foremen's parchment from the linen works, A.K. was presented with the freedom of the City of Perth. In March 1938, at the City Hall, Arthur Kinmond Bell and Lord Amulree were honoured by Perth, in A.K.'s case 'in recognition of the numerous benevolent and public services he had rendered to Perth'.

On that occasion he said, 'I have been twice across America, through a considerable part of Europe, and three times through Australia and New Zealand, and I have failed to find one spot which I would prefer to live in than our Fair City.'

As the *Perthshire Advertiser* said, 'His affection for Perth and his belief that a man who had the means should be prepared to spend money for the benefit of his native city were reflected in many munificent actions.'

The most famous of these was, of course, the Gannochy Trust, which has helped not only Perth but many other parts of Scotland.

The Inchgower distillery, Buckie, founded in 1871 and acquired by Bell's in 1936

A group of the directors and travelling staff of Bell's, 1936. Included are *Front left to right*, W. G. Farquharson (director), W. E. Anderson, A. K. Bell (managing director), A. Thomson (director), D. F. Forbes (director)
Back row, D. McKenzie, J. McRae, J. Hunter, J. Coonay, C. Thompson, R. Douglas, J. Ward, Wm Rollo, J. C. Ferguson, J. Gregory, C. D. Guy and D. A. Ainslie (director)

But A.K. was a great man for watching out for the little things and doing something about them. For example, he bought Quarrymill Den, a beauty spot on the outskirts of the city, and not only presented it to Perth but arranged for it to be looked after as well.

He thought allotment-holders in Perth were doing a good job, so he bought ground at Muirtown and Bellwood and presented it to them. On Moncreiffe Island in the river Tay he paid for the building of a pavilion as the headquarters of the Working Men's Garden Association. He helped the Perth Scouts and the Perth Old Men's Recreation Club and the Perth Silver Band Association. He was keen on music and joined in efforts to bring the best musicians, notably the B.B.C. Scottish Orchestra, to Perth.

But A.K. never forgot his business activities. He reported that in 1938 the export trade had been 'the most profitable part of our business'. At Leith they had 'constructed a large modern Washing and Bottling Department'. And there was sorrow over the death of Sandy Thompson, who had been secretary and director of Bell's for nearly fifty years.

Then, on 3 September 1939, the second World War broke out. One of the first casualties, as far as the home market was concerned, was the whisky trade. On the other hand, the export of whisky became of paramount importance in the war effort. The wartime slogan was 'Export or die'. The situation was expressed by A. K. Bell in the annual report presented in May 1940. 'As distilling has now practically stopped', he said, 'we have found it necessary, in order to conserve our stocks, to curtail our Home Sales by twenty per cent, and to cease meanwhile the development of the Home Market.'

It was the same message the following year. 'All that we can do is to carry on giving our Home Trade as high a quota as prudence dictates, keeping up our connections overseas, as well as assisting our country by full and regular shipments.'

A.K. took a deep interest in the progress of the war, and he kept an eagle eye on the way it was going in his native county. In July 1940 he wrote one of his famous letters, but this one was not to the Press. It was to General Sir Alan Brooke, London.

Sir,

I am of the opinion that you should be made aware of the appalling mistakes in connection with the war effort that have been and still are being made in Perth and Perthshire. I give you a few.

(1) A new Hangar was erected at the Perth Aerodrome with strong concrete floor. After erection it was discovered that this Hangar was not meant to be erected at Perth, but somewhere in Wales. It was accordingly taken to pieces and sent to Wales for erection there. The concrete floor could not be sent to Wales, and still is evidence of this mistake.

(2) A large hospital has been erected at Bridge of Earn, Perthshire, on low-lying ground near the River Earn, where in the last war a soldiers' camp stood. This camp had to be evacuated owing to the unhealthy and damp condition of the locality in winter. As it was found out that no adequate water supply was available for this hospital, roads have been hacked up and water brought from Glenfarg – some seven miles distant.

Seemingly it did not occur to those responsible that Glenfarg, which stands high, would have been a better site, with a water supply on the spot.

F

(3) For three weeks lately, a large squad of workers were employed in erecting poles over the Scone Racecourse on Lord Mansfield's estate, to prevent aeroplanes landing. A few days after this work was completed, another lot of workmen arrived and pulled up the poles referred to, and are engaged at present in cutting any trees on or adjoining the course, in order to make it suitable for aeroplanes landing.

(4) An embankment, to keep the River Almond from over-flowing when in flood, exists just before this river joins the Tay. A tank trench has been dug in this embankment with the result that one of the best farms in the district will be endangered the first time the Almond is in spate. I understand that this interference with the banks of the Almond has been stopped, but the portion already interfered with remains a danger.

Local contractors are already too busy to take on the work of filling in the trench, while to ask the Local Volunteers to fill it up again would not only discourage them but they would ask themselves, 'Are our services any real good to win this war, working under our present instructors?'

The trouble is that Perthshire does not seem to be singular,' and it is incredible that there are men in this country capable of such folly – or do they belong to the Fifth Column?

It is not only the loss involved in effort and money, but the confidence of the people is being undermined. We have always muddled through in the past, but if strict business methods are not adopted, and adopted quickly, we may try to muddle through once too often.

I am, yours faithfully,
A. K. Bell.

P.S. Since dictating this letter, I find that quite recently the concrete floor referred to in Paragraph (1) has been broken up to be used in bottoming a road!

A.K. was seventy years of age when he wrote that letter, but you can see that he was still alert and vigorous, and putting his peram-bulations around the countryside to good use. Unfortunately, there is no record as to whether or not General Sir Alan Brooke ever did more than acknowledge receipt of the letter.

The whisky business was in a peculiar position during the war.

A. K. Bell in later life

On the one hand, they were expected to sell whisky abroad and bring much needed money into the country. On the other, they were being deprived of the raw material from which the whisky was made. In the last report that he made at an annual general meeting of Bell's, A.K. had to announce a profit of nearly £100,000, but the three distilleries at Blair Athol, Inchgower and Dufftown were all showing trading losses.

In April 1942, A.K. seemed as vigorous as ever. The only luxury that he had ever allowed himself was a Rolls Royce. After he had walked round Gannochy, his chauffeur would drive him down into Perth. But, before the Rolls reached Victoria Street, A.K. would stop it and complete his journey to the office on foot. One Friday the driver was surprised when he called to collect the boss to be told that Mr Bell was unwell, but would let him know when next he would be needed. But he never received a summons, for A. K. Bell died on the following Sunday morning.

The people of Perth were surprised and sad to read in the *Perthshire Advertiser* of 29 April 1942 the headings – 'Sudden Death of Mr A. K. Bell. Perth Mourns One Of Its Greatest Benefactors.' The *Advertiser* said:

Perth has lost one of its greatest benefactors of all time. Mr Bell's love of his native city found expression in innumerable ways and he leaves behind him such a record of good deeds as it has been given to few men to perform.

The intimation that he had passed away came as a shock to his closest friends, whose profound sense of loss has been shared by the citizens in general. It was typical of a man of Mr Bell's tremendous vitality that he should be active until the last.

The Lord Provost of Perth, Sir John Ure Primrose, expressed the city's feelings when he wrote:

A. K. Bell loved the wide open spaces, and those of us who used to watch for his straight and agile figure, as he took his walk of a week-end up through Gannochy and on to Muirhall, will miss not only the sight of him, but the always interesting chats which revealed so clearly the interest which he took in his fellow-men, and the fine understanding he had of them. I know no man who did so much good with such little fuss, and with no thought of self-aggrandizement. There must be hundreds of people in Perth whom he befriended at a time in their lives when, but for his help and ready sympathy, life would have been very miserable indeed.

A.K. hated flattery and was, I think, even shy of thanks rendered to him for a kindness. He was, it is true, very strong-minded and gave to some people the impression of brusqueness, but there was no man who, if he found he had been wrong, admitted it more readily, and was so quick to make amends. His life was altogether wholesome and according to Nature, rejoicing in the sunshine and the gladness of the world. The heights of his Achievement were not indeed of Alpine altitudes, such as are climbed by the great and famous, but rather on the scale of his own beloved Scottish hills, comparatively unimposing, yet still hard to conquer.

He was happy in the opportunity of his death, for he was spared that which to him would have been a sore trial, years of weakness and disability. He remains part of our experience. Somewhere he is at work and walks abroad in sunshine.

With the death of Arthur Kinmond Bell, the second era of Bell's ended – in the middle of the greatest war in history, at a time of tragedy and, if not fear, a dreadful doubting.

6

The Edge of Circumstance

FROM a lifetime's experience of seeing industry from the outside, and writing about it too, I have come to the conclusion that the men who make a successful business tend to be larger-than-life characters. So it has been, and still is, with Bell's. The original Arthur Bell started in a very small way indeed but, according to his Victorian lights, was a man of determined views and considerable energy. His son, Arthur Kinmond Bell, was perhaps an even stronger character, and he built a strong, if still medium-sized business. He was eventually succeeded by the man who came into the firm as a young ex-soldier and chartered accountant, William Govan Farquharson, and he proved to be a strong man too.

When A. K. Bell died so suddenly, his younger brother, Robert D. Bell, was called from his life as a country gentleman to take over the position of managing director of Bell's. The appointment was known by all, including Robert Bell himself, as a temporary one, to bridge over the gap between A.K. and the next incumbent. Robert, as we have seen, was a pleasant, kindly man with no great taste for business, although he did know something about the blending of Bell's whisky. He was now seventy years of age and had not taken a direct interest in the affairs of the company for many years.

In the deliberations of those closely connected with the company one name came out quite easily at the top, and that was the name of W. G. Farquharson. And so Farquie was appointed chairman and managing director of Bell's. Robert Bell was happy to relinquish the position after one month. He was not a well man, and he died in the same year as his brother A. K. Bell. There are still people

Robert Duff Bell

connected with Bell's who talk of him as a happy-go-lucky character whose main aim in life was to enjoy himself, but I think I have made it clear that, when he wanted to work, Robert was a true Bell. With him the Bell family disappeared from the firm, although their name will always be connected with it.

Farquie took over in the perilous position of wartime. A. K. Bell died in April 1942, and it was W. G. Farquharson's job to present the report for 1941 at the annual general meeting of the company in May 1942. It was the same story of the falling Home Trade as compared with the rising Export Trade. 'Despite the quotas,' he said, 'which we have been able to obtain from the restricted amount of distilling carried on since 1940, it becomes more and more difficult to maintain stocks. This, along with rising costs, high Government duties and the loss of certain Colonial and Foreign Markets due to the war, makes our future trading uncertain.'

If you come to the conclusion that whisky makers live on the edge of circumstance, you are quite correct. They didn't know where their next enemy was coming from! Farquie was just getting into his stride as managing director when a quite unexpected problem arose. After A. K. Bell's death, there was trouble with the Death Duty branch of the Civil Service, who were assessing A.K.'s holding in the company at a figure which was completely crippling. A.K. had laid down whisky stocks years before at a price of 2s. 6d. a gallon for grain whisky and from 3s. 9d. to 4s. 6d. for the malt. The Death Duty people found that the figure per gallon on the open market, for grain as well as malt whisky was now £20. What they wanted to do was to assess the Death Duty on A. K. Bell's estate at this figure.

If this had been done, the results would have been disastrous. Bell's would have been forced to sell their valuable stocks and almost certainly would have gone out of business. W. G. Farquharson saw a way out. He contacted the Board of Trade, told them of the Death Duty problem, and pointed out that Bell's export trade, bringing in thousands of dollars to a wartime Britain which badly needed the money, would be ruined. The Board of Trade agreed heartily and now Farquie had two Government departments fighting each other! Fortunately, the Board of Trade won and Bell's didn't need to sell even a gill of whisky on the open market.

The difference between wartime and the days of peace are outlined by Jimmy Ward, a successful business man in Perth today,

William Govan Farquharson, managing director, and chairman of Bell's from 1942 to 1973

who was a salesman of Bell's whisky both under A. K. Bell and
W. G. Farquharson.

I started in 1935, and I was the first regular traveller for the
firm. Before that there was a chap called Bob Fyall who took
orders and then went out in his dungarees and delivered the
whisky on a barrow which he trundled round the pubs. When
I got the traveller's appointment, a man on the office staff
assured me, 'You're not doing Bob Fyall out of a job.'

In those days I was making 20 calls a day on pubs, hotels
and other customers. That meant taking 20 nips of whisky. By
3 p.m. I had the best part of a bottle of whisky inside me. Then
I went for lunch. Old A.K. didn't like the idea of his traveller
drinking and said to me, 'If you find you've got to drink to get
an order, don't go back.' Can you imagine? In my opinion a
teetotal whisky traveller couldn't have sold a box of matches
in those days.

Jimmy Ward suggested to the powers-that-be in Bell's that
there should be more travellers on the road and, just before the
war, there were a dozen men covering Scotland alone. But, when
the war broke out, there was little to sell in Scotland and most of
the men joined the Forces. Jimmy Ward went into the Royal Air
Force. 'A. K. Bell looked after us well,' he says. 'We were used to
getting the occasional bonus of shares. I remember one time even
the office boy got a free gift of 25 shares at £1 each. And, when we
were away during the war, A.K. saw that everybody in the Services
had his pay made up.

'Not only that, but he decided that there would be a welcome-
home gift of 2000 shares in the company for each of us. But you
know how suddenly he died. There was a stray cow in his garden
at Kincarrathie House and he went out in the pouring rain to chase
it out. He caught a chill and died in a couple of days. And that
meant he never signed the document that would have given the ex-
Servicemen 2000 shares each. They would have been worth about
£100,000 today!'

The days of travellers having to go out and sell whisky were over
for the time. It was a seller's market, as they say. In Britain whisky
was in short supply and in some cities the public houses had a system
by which a bell was rung to show that whisky was on sale. When
the bell stopped ringing, whisky was 'off'!

In Victoria Street, Perth, the Bell's people found that the job was not selling the whisky, but allocating it. The export trade was flourishing, on the other hand, and hardly a week passed without two or three letters coming in from countries all over the world asking for an agency for Bell's whisky.

There is a chart in Bell's office today which shows the expenses incurred by the firm for each year from 1937 to 1944, so it is easy to see at a glance what effect the war had. Although the staff went down, the salaries went up from £21,324 to £24,542. But travellers' salaries and expenses went down from £7903 to £4027. In the year before the war broke out, 1938, they had been £8494. Advertising expenses in 1938 came to £15,674. In 1944 all that Bell's were spending on advertisements was £3553.

On the other hand, Bad and Doubtful Debts were completely wiped out during the war years, a fact that the original Arthur Bell would undoubtedly have applauded.

By 1945 even the pessimists conceded that Britain, America and their Allies were likely to win the war in Europe, though Japan's declaration of war on the United States had meant a great deal of doubt about the future of the conflict in the Far East. At that time, of course, the vast majority of people knew nothing of the existence of the nuclear bomb which was going to bring the global war to such a sudden close in the following year.

In Britain the Government at least granted licences to all distillers, both malt and grain, permitting a limited amount of new distillation to take place during 1945. So Bell's were able to restart both their Dufftown-Glenlivet and the Inchgower distilleries and by the end of the year they were in production. Nothing could be done about Blair Athol at Pitlochry, however. There had been plans to start distilling there in 1939, but these were killed when the war broke out.

The new Government licences were for a production of approximately 45 per the cent of distillery make of 1938–9, so that the demand for whisky, particularly at home, still exceeded the available supplies.

But, as 1945 came into autumn, spirits were up generally, even if they were also in short supply in licensed premises! In American magazines Bell's were advertising, with the heading, 'R-R-Resoundingly Fine!', a picture showing bottles of their Royal Vat and Special Reserve whiskies, along with the typical Bell's bell, and a

...of the...the Office of War Information.
rtment. The consignment includes coffee
es their sent by the Government of Brazil
unoffi- for Sicilian hospitals and old peo-
al views ples' homes.
hey do

Waste fats make ammunition
Save them for your country. Give
them to your butcher and he will
give you red points in return.

R-R-RESOUNDINGLY FINE

BELL'S
ROYAL VAT

LIQUEUR BLENDED SCOTCH WHISKY
TWELVE YEARS OLD

BELL'S
BLENDED Scotch

SPECIAL RESERVE

BELL'S
SCOTCH WHISKY

Bell's Special Reserve Blended Scotch Whisky, 86 Proof.
Bell's Royal Vat Liqueur Blended Scotch Whisky, 86 Proof.
Products of Arthur Bell & Sons Ltd., Distillers, Perth, Perthshire, Scotland.
G. F. Heublein & Bro., Inc., Hartford 1, Conn., Sole U S. Agents

certain
itly say
t Indo-
much.
is with
enthu-
aid the
heard
hat the
igns on
French
ve been
what it

d
ticle by
iere to-
iid that
sponsi-
trustee-
iat "all
s recog-
organ-
elf gov-
ediately

author-
decide
or the
istance,
were, it
ve inde-

know
ida and
ast are
id that
General
best of
esident,

The advertisement for Bell's, 'R-R-Resoundingly
Fine' which appeared in The American Press in 1945

caption below which read, 'You will hear more of Bell's after the
Victory bells ring out all over the world.'

W. G. Farquharson decided to mark the coming victory by
applying for a Coat of Arms for the firm (see frontispiece). This was
granted by Sir Francis James Grant, the Lord Lyon King of Arms
in Edinburgh, and I feel I must repeat the magnificent words of
heraldry which describe it.

After telling the history of the firm in brief, the parchment ends:

The Petition having Prayed that We would Grant Our Licence
& Authority unto the said Company to bear and use such
Ensigns Armorial as might be found suitable and according to
the Laws of Arms: KNOW YE, therefore, that We have Devised
and Do by These Presents Assign, Ratify and Confirm unto the
said ARTHUR BELL AND SONS Limited the following
Ensigns Armorial as depicted upon the margin hereof and
matriculated of even date with These Presents upon the forty-
Third folio of the Thirty-fifth Volume of Our Public Register of
All Arms and Bearings in Scotland, Videlicet: – *Vert, a bell Or.*
Above the shield is placed an helmet of befitting Degree with a
Mantling Vert doubled Or, and on a Wreath of the Liveries is
set for Crest: – *the sun rising Or.* On a Compartment below the
shield with this Motto – NUNC ET SEMPER are set for
Supporters – *two lions Gules, armed and fanged Azure.* In
Testimony whereof These Presents are subscribed by Us and the
Seal of Our Office is Affixed hereto at Edinburgh on the
Twenty-fifth day of June in the Ninth Year of the Reign of
Our Sovereign Lord George the Sixth, by the Grace of God,
of Great Britain, Ireland and the British Dominions beyond the
Seas, King, Defender of the faith, Emperor of India, etc., and
in the Year of Our Lord, One Thousand Nine Hundred and forty-
five.

The end of the war inspired one author to write a poem on
'Scotland's Outstanding Scotch' and, since Bell's seems to inspire
poets, I give it here:

> Land of the mountains, the lakes and the dells,
> Land of Scotch Whisky distilled there by Bell's.
> Scotland's outstanding the quality blend,
> A great-hearted Whisky – a bonnie wee friend.
> Look where you may in each country or clime,
> Bell's famous Whisky is mellowed by time.
>
> Land of the crofters, the clans and the glen
> Where Whisky is Whisky to brave hardy men,
> The men who know values to Scotland endears
> Bell's proud reputation for many past years.
> The pride of the Highlands and Lowlands, ye ken,
> This outstanding Scotch is the password for men.

In the long winter nights may we oft raise a glass
Of this excellent blend, a real Whisky of class,
And recall perhaps memories of times that we knew
With our backs to the wall – and the First of the Few,
And a friend there to warm us in those hectic spells
Was a great-hearted Whisky – the product of Bell's.

May the Rose and the Thistle forever entwine
Where the Land of the Mountains greets your hand and mine.
Good Health and Good Fortune, these I would foretell
In a glass of 'Real Scotland' distilled by 'A Bell'.

Well, if the poetry and the English are doubtful, the sentiments, at least, are irreproachable.

The Path to Peace

MEMORY, as we all know, plays us some strange tricks. Many people who went through the last war are quite convinced, in retrospect, that things returned to normal in a year or two. It wasn't like that at all. Rationing and utility clothing and furniture was our lot for a long time. As far as the making of whisky was concerned, it was fully twelve years before the level of distilling in Scotland approached the pre-war days.

The Government at that time seemed to be playing a cat-and-mouse game with the distillers. As I have said, in 1945 distilling was allowed up to 45 per cent of the 1938–9 makes. But no distilling licences were granted at all by the Ministry of Food in 1946. There was a partial resumption of distilling in 1947, but Bell's announced, 'The Government has now decided that, as from 1st May, 1947, the Home Market will only be permitted approximately 25 per cent supplies of the datum year, 1939–40, and the balance of 75 per cent will be exported, the greater part of which will go to the Hard Currency Markets. As your company in the past enjoyed a large measure of its trade from the Home Market, this will be seriously affected by the new arrangement.'

Of course, there was another side to the coin. Although both Arthur Bell and A.K. had said brave words about Bell's export trade, it was a small one compared with some of the other whisky companies. It was during and just after the war that Farquie was given the opportunity to expand the export business and he took it. The expansion today is far ahead of what happened then, but it was started at that time.

As peace progressed, however, Farquie thought he should get the

Bell's distilleries in readiness for the future boom. By this time
Jimmy Ward had been demobilized from the Royal Air Force and
had rejoined the staff at Victoria Street. He was now officially
designated as the Home Trade Sales Manager. The title was impressive, but the fact was that he had practically nothing to sell
to the home trade. So, when Farquie decided to concentrate on the
distilleries, and particularly his favourite Blair Athol, Jimmy Ward
found that he was spending more time accompanying the managing
director around than he was on his own alleged job.

They went first of all to their Inchgower Distillery at Buckie.
I should point out that a fine big volume entitled *Moray and Banff
Illustrated* had a special piece on Inchgower and placed it 'by
Fochabers, Banffshire'. Inchgower Distillery is much nearer Buckie
than Fochabers, but Fochabers is a resort of the élite, the hunters
and the anglers, while Buckie is a down-to-earth – or maybe down-
to-sea would be a better description – place which might not have
appealed to the Edwardian readers for whom *Moray and Banff
Illustrated* was intended.

Its pellucid prose is worth repeating. 'The neighbourhood of
Fochabers,' it said, 'has many things to attract attention and compel admiration. The splendid mansion of Gordon Castle, the noble
railway viaduct over the Spey, and, above all, the magnificent
natural scenery with the distant heights of Benrinnes, Benaigen,
and Corriehabbie, standing out against the clear blue sky, are
attractions of no common order, that might well defy the pen of
the ablest writer to describe.'

But this able writer is not perturbed. He goes on:

However, our business in this article is of a more practical
character. It is to say a few words on the Inchgower distillery,
one of the noted seats of production of the famous Highland
Malt Whisky for which the valley of the Spey has such a distinctive *celebrity*. This distillery is not amongst the oldest in the
district, but its productions have a reputation of the first order,
and in construction and equipment it is modelled on improved
modern lines.

In local surroundings also it is exceptionally favoured, the
quality and purity of the water, as well as the purity of the
atmosphere, being specially favourable to the production of
choice whisky.

Inchgower Distillery was founded in 1870 and it has still a fine Victorian feeling about it, although Bell's have introduced modern methods and increased production considerably. When Farquie and Jimmy Ward visited it, distilling had restarted, but there was still a slight air of A.K.'s statement in 1937 that 'as the bonding accommodation at this Distillery is altogether in excess of requirements, Messrs Bell have converted one of the largest bonds into a general warehouse. Buckie being within reasonable distance of the Glenlivet District, and the Warehouse in such close proximity to Buckie harbour, the site of this bond is ideal for those Distillers in the District referred to who, owing to the present activity in the distilling industry, are finding it hard to provide the necessary bonding accommodation for their makes. This large bond having no upper storey – all confined to the ground floor – should prove excellent for the maturing of Whisky.' You'll notice that A.K. didn't mention Fochabers. He knew – none better since he had bought the place – that it was by Buckie.

Indeed, the water which gave Inchgower malt its distinctive taste came from the Hill of Minduff, two and a half miles away, and was once Buckie's water supply as well as the distillery's.

The great man around Inchgower is Ned Shaw, now retired but for long enough manager of the distillery. Ned is namely in the North for his wit and his fund of strange stories. He has appeared on both radio and television. He has been involved in the making of whisky for more than fifty years, and he remembers the days when work in a distillery was a hard, back-breaking job. There was, of course, no mechanical handling in his day and everything that was moved had to be moved by sheer muscle. He remembers, too, the time when a whisky vat was cleaned by men wielding heather besoms. And even when the effluent from the whisky-making was drained into a convenient burn, and he washed the stones round the water to remove the tell-tale traces of whisky effluent.

'The great whisky drinkers in my time,' says Ned Shaw, 'had their own special way of tasting the stuff. They'd take a dram of whisky first and then some water, and shoogle the mixture around in their mouth!'

Most of the workers in Inchgower were from the very individual town of Buckie, a place with a sharp tang of its own. One of them, when remonstrated with for drinking too much on the job, replied indignantly, 'And why no'? I've been lang enough kept doon in this warld!'

G

The Dufftown-Glenlivet distillery

Then there was the chap who dropped in occasionally to Inch-gower to see how things were getting on and always made an excuse for a dram – he was cold or thirsty or had a hangover or his auntie had died or his shinty team had lost, or whatever. One day the manager saw him approaching Inchgower and forestalled him. He gave him a dram before the excuser could give his excuse. Then the manager said, 'What's the reason this time?' 'Well,' said the visitor, 'I was thinking on the way here of a good excuse, but now that I've got my dram, it'll do for another time!'

However, if you ask Ned Shaw what his most remarkable experience in distilling has been, he'll tell you that it was when Bell's decided to convert their coal furnaces to steam distillation. 'Oh, we fairly had our teething troubles,' he says, 'and we nearly went back to coal.'

But W. G. Farquharson was the man who decided to convert from coal to steam and he would not be moved. As usual, he was proved right.

From Inchgower Farquie and Jimmy Ward continued their tour to Dufftown-Glenlivet. What they saw at the distillery there some thirty years ago they would still see today, except for some very important internal changes. The distillery lies in a little ravine through which the Dullan Water runs. There is still a water mill, but it has not worked for many years. But when I was there last, I saw a heron on one of the boulders in the burn.

The water which gives Dufftown-Glenlivet malt whisky its special (and highly regarded) taste does not come from the Dullan Water, however. It is piped from the Highlandman's Well in the Conval Hills some miles away. The Dullan Water provides power, as it did in the days when there were a saw mill and a meal mill on its banks at this precise spot. The distillery took over these mills in 1896 and rebuilt the place.

Dufftown-Glenlivet, you may recollect, was bought from the firm of Peter Mackenzie by A. K. Bell in 1933. It was a very good buy, and Farquie made it better by bringing in surrounding ground. The result was that Bell's not only owned the distillery, and a dozen cottages, but also the extensive lands of Pittyvaich Farm, Pittyvaich Woodlands and Pittyvaich Shootings. As we shall see later, these lands were to prove very important indeed in the development of Bell's today.

When A. K. Bell took over Peter Mackenzie's business in 1933 he also acquired the Blair Athol Distillery at Pitlochry, which could well be called the centre of the Scotch distilling industry, since Pitlochry happens to be the geographical centre of Scotland. It's not a romantic idea but just the truth that, when William Govan Farquharson saw the place, he fell in love with it. It was Farquie's ideal distillery. Like all tough men, he was a romantic at heart and Blair Athol was full of romance and excitement.

First of all, parts of the present building go back 250 years and it's quite possible that the distilling of whisky was taking place even then. Nobody knows how old whisky is, but there is a theory that the Picts were making it in Scotland before anybody else thought of it. The burn of Allt Dour ('The Burn of the Otter') runs through the distillery and provides the water for whisky making. Originally it would run through the grounds of the farm of Allt Dour, called Aldour today and part of the Blair Athol Distillery complex.

Certainly Allt Dour has had its place in history. After the Duke of Cumberland had defeated Bonnie Prince Charlie's Highland Army at Culloden in 1740, a fugitive from the battle came carefully back to his calf country. He was a local laird, Robertson of Faskally, the place where the man-made Loch Faskally ripples today. He knew that the Government red-coats were not far behind him. They had orders to capture every Highland officer they could and kill him if necessary. So Robertson avoided his home at Faskally, and made for the farmhouse of Allt Dour. There he was welcomed and found shelter.

But soon word came that Cumberland's men had arrived at Pitlochry and were searching for Robertson. They were, in fact, closing in on the farmhouse of Allt Dour from either side. Robertson ran from the farmhouse to the burn and crawled down below its banks to what is called today the Irrigation Meadow. He knew there was an ancient oak there whose branches would make a good hiding place. He climbed the tree and remained hidden there until the red-coats decided there was no more point in searching for him and made south.

He went back to Allt Dour, doubtless had a thanksgiving glass of the home-made usquebaugh, and later escaped across country to the east coast and got a boat to France, the favourite destination of all fleeing Jacobites.

This old Atholl oak tree is still down the road not many yards from the Blair Athol Distillery and is supposed to be something like four hundred years old by this time. Farquie liked the Robertson story, but he liked even more the tale of the distiller who cheated the Government. Who wouldn't?

Towards the end of last century the proprietor of Blair Athol Distillery, long before Peter Mackenzie took over, decided on a plan to make some extra money. He brought his head worker into the scheme and between them they made a hole in one of the Government's bonded warehouses in the grounds. Then, at dead of night, they pumped a huge amount of whisky out of the warehouse and into casks, for illegal disposal later. This meant that they were releasing the whisky without duty, which is a dreadful crime, as any Exciseman will tell you.

But there was a leak somewhere. The distiller learned that the story had got to Government sources and that their minions were on his track. Indeed, there were detectives watching him and preparing to pounce. Perhaps he thought of climbing the Robertson

The Blair Athol distillery, Pitlochry

Oak and waiting until they had gone. But maybe he rejected the idea because it had been tried already. Anyway, he thought of a much more ingenious plan.

The Highland railway ran through Pitlochry, as it still does under the name of British Rail, and it was a single line except at important stations, where it was a double line within the confines of the station. Pitlochry Station was important enough to have a double line, where the southbound train had to pass the train going north. Knowing that he was being followed by the two detectives, the distiller went from Blair Athol Distillery to Pitlochry Station and boarded the train going north. The detectives did the same, but naturally sat in a different compartment so that their quarry would not know that he was being tailed.

Then in came the southbound train from Inverness and lined up alongside the train for the north. There was always an appreciable

amount of time before one or the other started running again, and
the peccable distiller chose the right moment to get out of his compartment, steal over the bridge and get into the train going south.
He laid low and eventually the detectives steamed north while the
distiller travelled south. And that is all anybody knows of the
story, because he never came back to Pitlochry again.

When Farquie saw Blair Athol he was undoubtedly impressed
by its history, but he was not impressed by its appearance. It was
a long time since whisky had been distilled there and the place had
been allowed to lapse into desuetude. He engaged an elderly architect from Edinburgh to prepare plans for the renovation of Blair
Athol, and this gentleman was a traditionalist. He had no time for
what was then the modern trend for glass and chromium. This suited
Farquie, who was always out for the best. According to Jimmy
Ward, Farquie was a perfectionist and 'First class was good enough
—just!'

In the course of their· travels around Bell's three distilleries,
Farquie and Jimmy Ward arrived at Blair Athol in time to inspect
the wall of the still-house, facing the main road leading into
Pitlochry. The workmanship on this. wall did not please Farquie at
all and he immediately sacked the builder. Then he engaged a new
builder and ordered him to pull down the new wall and build a
newer one. Everybody connected with the rebuilding of Blair Athol
had a bad time, and the day came when Farquie arrived to look
over the final result.

'It's a real show piece,' said the irrepressible Jimmy Ward.

'So it should be,' said Farquie, who was looking rather worried.
'It's cost well over £75,000.'

'Well,' said Jimmy, 'I think the day's not very far distant when
you'll be boasting to your friends that that's all it cost you.'

Farquie's face lit up and he said, 'Jimmy, you've made my day!'

Jimmy Ward says now, 'I didn't really feel any happier than
Farquie did. I'd been told that, between wages, malted barley,
power and a few other things, Blair Athol was going to cost £1000
a week, and it would be at least three years, maybe more, before
we would know whether the whisky would be any good or not. Ah,
well, it was a calculated gamble which paid very handsome
dividends.'

In fact, distilling started at Blair Athol in November, 1949, and
has been outstandingly successful ever since, It is one of the show

The Perth–Dundee railway line, an escape route for
an errant distiller

pieces of Bell's set-up and people from all over the world have
visited the distillery. Indeed, it is one of the tourist attractions of
Pitlochry and comes second only to the Pitlochry Festival Theatre
in attracting the crowds.

In 1949 the firm of Arthur Bell and Sons was converted from a
private into a public company. The directors were named as
William Govan Farquharson, C.A., Scotch Whisky Distiller;
Donald Mackay, Solicitor; and David Arthur Ainslie, also a Scotch
Whisky Distiller. It was explained in the Stock Exchange pros-
pectus that 'The Company requires additional Capital, largely
because it has recently had to repay sums amounting to approxi-
mately £247,000 which were held on loan from the late Mr A. K.
Bell (who was the founder of the Company in its modern form, and
who died in 1942) and members of his family. In addition the
Company has to provide approximately £54.000 for essential
Distillery reconstruction work.'

1.   The combined profits of the Group for the ten years ending 31st December, 1947, arrived at on the basis of the audited accounts adjusted as explained below, and the dividends paid by the parent Company, were as follows :—

(1) Year ended 31st Dec.	(2) Combined Profits as defined below.	(3) Wear and Tear and Initial allowances.	(4) N.D.C., E.P.T. and Profits Tax (Provisional).	(5) Net Profits before charging Income Tax.	(6) Ordinary Dividend Rate per cent., *less* Tax.	(7) Preference Dividend Rate per cent., *less* Tax.
	£	£	£	£		
1938	82,393	942	4,172	77,279	20	8
1939	90,470	1,138	6,639	82,693	20	8
1940	83,050	1,353	933	80,764	20	8
1941	94,612	1,339	8,336	84,937	20	8
1942	115,692	1,235	34,922	79,535	20	8
1943	114,988	1,134	35,935	77,919	20	8
1944	111,192	987	33,563	76,642	20	8
1945	116,429	892	39,800	75,737	25	8
1946	138,660	913	*36,000	101,747	25	8
1947	154,375	1,782	*23,561	129,032	25	8

*Estimated.

Bell's combined profits for the ten years ending 31 December 1947

The value of the firm at that date was estimated by the Auditors to be £680,740, but it was emphasized that 'The Whisky stocks are included in the Company's accounts at cost or market value, whichever is lower. *These stocks have, however, a value several times higher than their book value.*' The Share Capital came to £267,698.

It was proposed that the new Share Capital of the public company should be authorized at £650,000, but the actual issue should be £600,000, made up of £400,000 in 4½ per cent Cumulative Preference Shares of £1 each, and £200,000 in Ordinary Shares of £1 each.

All seemed to be sweetness and light at that time, but you must never judge things by the surface appearance. There was trouble at the Auchtermuchty bonded warehouse. A large amount of whisky disappeared inexplicably from Auchtermuchty. The police were put on the trail. At first they had no success, but then, when a woodland fire broke out on the outskirts of Dunfermline, most of the stolen whisky was discovered.

One cask was still missing, and it might have been missing forever if an astute policeman in the picture-book village of Culross had not noted that one well-known inhabitant of the town seemed to be always 'under the influence', and yet never went near any of the hostelries in the place. One day the police raided certain premises in Culross and they found the cask, with a much reduced amount of whisky inside it, buried under a horse-drawn hearse!

Ex.-R.S.M. Ronald Brittain presenting Mrs W. G. Farquharson with a golden bell of flowers at a press conference which Mr W. G. Farquharson (right) gave in London on the eve of their departure for the United States.

Bell's, as most people know, have always been a completely independent company, although there were times, particularly in A.K.'s latter days, when very tempting offers were made for a take-over. But A.K. resolutely refused even to consider such offers. He was determined on independence, and Farquie followed the same lines. Even today, in spite of various pressures, Bell's remains independent.

There was a time when Bell's biggest competitors reduced the age of their blends and this made it possible for them to sell some extra cases to their customers. It was suggested to Farquie that Bell's should follow the lead of their competitors by reducing the ages of the whiskies in the blend and so increase their sales. Farquie was downright in his refusal even to countenance such a thing. He said he would never reduce the quality of Bell's blends. Moreover, he said he thought the publicans' threats were groundless, since the quality of Bell's whisky would force them to stock it because of popular demand. It need only be said that he was proved right.

In the fifties W. G. Farquharson, accompanied by his wife, started a series of journeys round the world, with the object of making

TOLD BY BELL'S   NO. 1.

They flayed

him alive . . .

It was in 900 A.D. The Danes had sailed up the River Severn, in Western England, and raided the City of Worcester. One Viking, not content with ordinary loot, had stayed behind to steal the Sanctus bell from the Cathedral. It was heavy. He managed to lower it to the ground, but it was a job to get it on his back and stagger off with it. Whilst he was trying to do this the city people returned and literally 'caught him bending' beneath the weight of the bell. Furious and outraged, the monks and citizens fell upon the sacrilegious thief and soon flayed him alive. Then they tanned his skin and nailed it to the inner side of the great West doors of the Cathedral, as a warning to others. Parts of the skin can be seen on the door to this day!

*   *   *   *

The bells of Britain have a long, sometimes lurid history. In another way, Bell's of Scotland have their history too. But it is a happy history of careful distilling and blending to make a famous whisky. When you want a smooth, mature Scotch whisky — ring for Bell's!

BELL'S

OLD SCOTCH

WHISKY

AFORE YE GO —

Distilled, blended and bottled by

ARTHUR BELL & SONS LTD., *Distillers, of Perth, Scotland. Estd. 1825*

Bell's even better known abroad. He was a very good ambassador for Bell's in a social sense, and must have influenced the export of whisky considerably.

At the same time it must be said that he had spent his time, since he became managing director of Bell's, in a sellers' market and not a buyers' one, and perhaps he never quite adjusted himself to the change. His forte lay in administration, in the search for perfection, and in the laying down of fine malt whiskies. This last was to prove of inestimable value to Bell's in time to come.

Meanwhile, however, Bell's continued to make progress. In 1951 their profits reached well over £250,000. In 1952 the cost of their advertising was more than £57,000, a figure that would have been far beyond Arthur Bell's comprehension, and would even have worried A.K., because it was bigger than most of his profits.

Certainly when Farquie went on his travels around the world, he had plenty of countries keen on whisky to choose from. In a detailed list of Bell's export sales for the year 1953, some 84 countries are mentioned, including such possibly unexpected ones as Aruba, Angola, Curaçao, Fiji, Iceland, Lebanon, Morocco, Grenada, Russia (in 1953!), St Kitts, and Turkey. But it must be admitted that the quantity of whisky sold to some of these places was very small indeed. Russia's total, for example, amounted to exactly £100. Turkey's was a mere £92. The lowest was St Kitts, which came to all of £40. There was no mention at all, by the way, of either Manchuria or China, so the enterprising Mr de Haas of Rotterdam must have failed in his proposed efforts to convert the Manchurians and the Chinese into Bell's whisky drinkers at that time.

The big-timers, so to speak, in the 1951 list were Australia (£34,920), Canada (£24,146), Chile (£11,041), New Zealand (£66,928), South Africa (£97,450), Southern Rhodesia (£31,420), India (£21,330), and, towering above all the rest, the United States of America (£372,124). All of these figures, incidentally, are modest indeed compared with Bell's exports today.

Although the Second World War had been over for more than eight years, the home market was getting only 20 per cent of Bell's production of whisky. But, owing to Government taxation, people in Britain paid £611,873 for this 20 per cent, while the lucky export countries paid only £825,267 for 80 per cent of the Scotch whisky produced by Bell's. This was, perhaps, tolerated when 'there was a

An advertisement from Bell's 1951–2 campaign

war on', but the public, particularly in Scotland, irked more and more at the situation where you could get unlimited whisky at a cheap price as long as you were outside the country in which the stuff was made!

The Government, as all Governments do, gradually reduced their grip on the home trade of the Scotch distillers. But it was not until 1958, some thirteen years after the war had ended in Europe, that the imbalance was corrected, and the home market came into its own once again. And it was about this time that the fourth larger-than-life figure (and I am expressing my own view in these descriptions) joined Bell's and started to carve his way to control. His name was Raymond C. Miquel, and with him we go into the next era in the story of Bell's hundred and fifty years.

The Coming Man

THE story of the 150 years, so far, of Bell's whisky falls naturally into four parts – the early times first controlled by the original Arthur Bell, followed by the more expansive field envisaged by his son, Arthur Kinmond Bell, and then the unusual wartime conditions faced by William Govan Farquharson. Fourthly there came a young man who had not been brought up in the whisky tradition at all, but he knew where he was going.

Raymond Miquel, the newcomer on the scene of Bell's whisky, was born in London in 1931. His father was French, and Raymond's early boyhood was spent in the Channel Islands. At the beginning of the war the Miquel family moved back to London and then, in 1943, when Raymond was twelve years of age, they flitted north to Glasgow. The boy was sent to one of Glasgow's most famous schools, Allan Glen's, named after the shipbuilder who started life as a poor boy and eventually put up the money to build the original academy.

Raymond as a boy had two loves in his live – sport and making enough money to be able to continue his sporting life. He was keen on football, tennis and rowing, and to make certain that he could finance his sporting activities he sold comic papers in Allan Glen's playground and sometimes of an evening worked as an assistant in a snooker parlour in Glasgow. These extra-mural activities did not interfere with his scholastic work, however, and he did particularly well in the field of mathematics.

He had some embryonic ideas about becoming an architect, but in those days, though the Second World War was ended by the time he was due to leave school, National Service was automatic.

Raymond C. Miquel

So he went into the Royal Air Force, and he looks back today on that time as his substitute for a University. There are many widely differing views on the value or otherwise of National Service, but one thing I feel is true, and that is that it gave one an experience of life, discipline and contact with one's fellow men and women. What Raymond Miquel remembers best about his days in the R.A.F. was the way his fellow 'erks' and he spent long hours in debating the future.

When he was released from the Royal Air Force and came back to Glasgow, Raymond Miquel was still interested in becoming an architect. But the salary offered to him as an apprentice with an architect's firm was £2 10s. a week. When he discovered that he could earn £6 a week on the staff of P.E. Management Consultants, he had no hesitation in giving up his architectural ideas. The Management Consultants sent him to a knitwear factory in Glasgow for training in time and motion study and accounting. He did well and in two years his salary had risen to £9 a week. He found it difficult to keep up such communal sporting activities as football, tennis and rowing and in his spare time he went in for running, a sport which you can carry out entirely by yourself if there are no other runners around. Almost every night of the week Raymond Miquel, when he had finished work, went out on a ten-mile run.

In 1956 Raymond Miquel learned that there was a job going for an 'efficiency expert' at the Leith warehouse of Arthur Bell and Sons, Ltd. He applied and was summoned to an interview at Bell's office in Perth. There for the first time he met the formidable figure of W. G. Farquharson. It turned out that what Farquie wanted was a works study engineer and following the interview he offered the job to Raymond Miquel. The young man said he was interested, but that he felt he ought to see the plant before he decided whether or not to take the job. So it was arranged that he should have a conducted tour of the warehouse complex at Leith.

Now I feel at this point that it must be said that there are many people in the world of whisky who have been brought up in the tradition that there is nothing wrong with primitive conditions in the places in which whisky is produced. I am not suggesting that these conditions necessarily apply today, but I have been visiting distilleries, bottling plants, blending houses, cooperages and the like for a wheen of years now, and I have seen some queer sights. I recall one famous distillery where the roofs were so low that you could only come to the conclusion that they were made for Snow White and the Seven Dwarfs – who may well have been operating a secret still for all I know.

The people who worked in places like that were not dissatisfied. They were used to these conditions. Sometimes they actually liked them, and resisted change. There are some marvellous new distilleries in Scotland today, but there are still the old hands who shake their heads and say that things aren't what they used to be and all this modern stuff is the beginning of the end of whisky.

This must be said at this point in my story, because Raymond Miquel had not been brought up in any whisky tradition and didn't even know what to expect. When he was shown round Bell's warehouses in Leith he was astonished. 'I thought I'd gone back into the Middle Ages,' he says now. 'I didn't think people worked like that in 1956. It was like a series of dungeons, with practically no light coming through the barred windows. Most of the doors were padlocked outside. It was incredible. When I went into the bottling plant I even found one of the girls sitting on a cushion on the floor because there was nowhere else for her to sit.'

In spite of what he had seen, Raymond Miquel decided to take the job, and so changed not only his own life but the way that Bell's would be run one day. He was given a small office in the Leith building and also a kindly admonition from William Govan Farquharson who said that his motto, in the best Bell's tradition, should be 'Hasten slowly'. The managing director took a good view of the energetic young man. Possibly Raymond Miquel reminded Farquie of his own energetic youth. And it was just as well that Farquie did like the new boy, because he was looked on with suspicion by quite a lot of the workpeople in the warehouse.

When, for example, he decided to time the operation of bottle-capping, there were some dark looks and a certain amount of muttering. 'Time and motion study' were bad words in those days.

Even when it came to the apparently simple operation of moving the Bell's lorries in and out of the narrow lane which ran round the group of buildings, there was trouble. Raymond Miquel studied the problem and realised that the solution was one-way traffic. So he worked out a system by which motor lorries should run in smoothly to unload and go round the lane when they had been reloaded. It should have all gone like clockwork.

BELL'S

ARTHUR BELL & SONS LTD DISTILLERS, PERTH, SCOTLAND.

ESTABLISHED 1825

v 'Afore Ye Go'

Scotch Whisky in the Making

VI   Whisky in the making

VII   The still house

But, on the first afternoon that the new method for the time and motion of motor lorries was to be carried out, Raymond Miquel was sitting in his wee office, working hard, when the warehouse manager's voice was heard. In stentorian tones he shouted, 'Raymond! Come here and see this bloody mess, Raymond!'

Raymond joined the manager at a window overlooking the lane. They gazed down on a scene of complete chaos. Some lorries were facing each other, others were at strange angles, and one or two more were rapidly approaching to add to the tangle. The manager waved his hand at the mixter-maxter and said, 'That's what comes of changing the way they've always worked.'

It didn't take long for Raymond Miquel to discover that this scene had been specially staged to teach him the error of his ways.

Next he came up against one of his biggest problems – the label situation. Most people don't realize the importance of labels on whisky bottles. Many places abroad have got exact requirements which must be met on the whisky label. Sometimes there are Government restrictions. Or it may be a particular whim of one of the customers. Bell's had to deal with some 600 different specifications and, though a layman might need a magnifying glass to see the difference between one whisky label and another, it was that difference that counted to the customer.

Only one man in the Leith warehouse knew all the labels. When a consignment had to go out with a label that hadn't been used for some time, the person in charge of this operation had to go to the label expert for supplies. There was then a long lapse of time while he tried to remember where he had put this particular label. Apparently he stored hundreds of labels in one of the six buildings which made up the blending and bottling complex, scores in another, and maybe one or two in a third. The whole bottling operation was held up while he debated on which building this label was in. Sometimes a search party was necessary before the all important label was found.

These were the kind of problems which Raymond Miquel faced in his efforts to bring some efficiency into the Leith operation. At the same time that he was tackling them, he was going to evening classes in Glasgow three nights a week, playing tennis, and keeping up his running. He ran anything up to one hundred miles a week, and gained a certificate which showed that he had completed the most arduous race in Britain, up to the top of Ben Nevis, the

H

BEN NEVIS RACE ASSOCIATION

𝕿his Certificate is presented to:

R. MIQUEL

of   GLASGOW

and certifies that he took part in the

BEN NEVIS RACE
OF 19 57

and completed the course in Two hours 32 minutes 10 seconds

Hon. Secretary.

Date 7th September, 1957   BEN NEVIS RACE ASSOCIATION

The certificate awarded to Raymond Miquel following
his completion of the Ben Nevis Race, 1957

highest mountain in the United Kingdom, and back down again.
Not only that, but his daily schedule as far as Leith was concerned
meant getting a train from Glasgow to Edinburgh at 5.30 a.m., and
one back at 7 p.m. No wonder he talks about discipline.

Gradually, in this exciting but odd life, Raymond Miquel
achieved some of his objects. For one thing, he got the ever-closed
windows open in the Leith warehouse. Just for a bonus he had new
lighting installed. He introduced stock-keeping. There had been no
stock-keeper in Leith before he arrived there. He found that the
bottling plant was not meeting a proper work schedule and in a
year he had cut the number of people working in it from sixty to
thirty-five. In that same year he showed a saving of £25,000 on
operations. In 1956 Leith turned out 300,000 cases of whisky.
Bell's now sell more than 3,000,000 cases each year.

In 1958 two important things happened to Raymond Miquel. He was married, and his boss, the great William Govan Farquharson himself, invited him to join the company at their headquarters in Victoria Street, Perth. He was to be given the job of examining the administration methods of the company. Victoria Street, by modern standards, was a somewhat outdated headquarters for a firm with the potential of Bell's but it was a great deal better than the warehouses at Leith.

Marriage sometimes tames a man, and it must be admitted that Raymond Miquel soon became accustomed to coming home at night and finding a meal and a chair waiting for him. Under these circumstances, his running dropped from around 100 miles a week to about 40. He was not doing so well in competitive running, but he was doing very well in the running of Bell's. So he gave up the other running.

At Perth he admired W. G. Farquharson's great knowledge of the whisky business, but he wondered if Bell's were adjusting fast enough to the change from a sellers' market to a buyers' market. On one occasion Miquel said to Farquie, 'I don't see any reason why Bell's shouldn't reach a profit of a million pounds a year.' Farquie said sternly to this irresponsible youngster, 'I'll never live to see the day when we'll make a million pounds a year.'

However, things were much easier in the home trade and Raymond Miquel made up an organization chart to show how deliveries could be improved. He suggested a form of production control, a one-day service locally, and a service to England the day after an English order came in. This was revolutionary, especially at a time such as Christmas. The time for closing down at Perth on Christmas Eve was five o'clock. But Raymond Miquel had a different idea. 'You work till every customer is satisfied,' he said. Otherwise, at Christmas time especially, a delivery could be delayed for about five days. So the workers at Perth stayed late, and it was the Custom and Excise men who complained about being made to work overtime. Eventually it was agreed that, on occasions like these, the closing time should be seven o'clock.

By this time Raymond Miquel had moved through various aspects of the company's activities. Farquie was casting an approving eye on him, and Miquel himself was keen on stepping up in Bell's hierarchy. But he couldn't see any opportunity at that time, as the youngest director of the firm disagreed with many of the

Kincarrathie House, after its conversion into a home
for old folk

ideas which he was putting forward. Then, unexpectedly, this
director left Bell's to join another company, leaving the way open
for Raymond Miquel. In 1962 he was invited by Farquie to join the
board of directors. And one year later Bell's profits exceeded the
amount which Farquie said he'd never live to see – £1,000,000. As
Punch would say, 'Collapse of stout party!'

The new director investigated the home sales force and found it
practically didn't exist. There were few salesmen and they averaged
only a dozen calls a day, as compared with Jimmy Ward's twenty a
day before the war. He started reorganizing and in just over a year
was able to hold the first meeting of the home sales group, considerably enlarged and doing well.

New plans were made for bottling plants to take over from the antediluvian Leith outfit. Farquie and Raymond Miquel toured the whole of Scotland looking for suitable sites. Farquie was still the perfectionist and, after he'd agreed that a certain place was the right one, he'd change his mind. 'We must have visited every county in Scotland, looking for sites,' recalls Raymond Miquel ruefully.

The idea, too, was to double the production of the three Bell's distilleries and this meant putting in two new stills where there were already two old ones. The traditionalists shook their heads They could advance plenty of instances when a distillery had been 'improved' and the result had been a complete difference in the quality of the whisky. This kind of talk is very difficult to counter-act, because nobody knows whether the story, told with such verisimilitude, is true or not. The only point I would make is that Bell's distilleries were doubled in plant and nobody has detected the slightest difference in the three whiskies.

Farquie was chairman of the Gannochy Trust and, while he did not in the least abate his concentration in the running of Bell's, he took a very personal interest in the Trust's affairs. He was very worried about the welfare of aged people. The Trust had decided to turn A. K. Bell's former home, Kincarrathie House, into a home for old folk. Farquie said, 'The greatest fear that aged people have is that their money will evaporate before they die.' His idea was that the old people who came into Kincarrathie should have this fear banished.

So he arranged that, when an elderly person applied for entrance, he or she would be charged a quite uneconomic rent, but the Gannochy Trust would have the power to claim something from their estate when they died. Farquie was always a man of the world, and it was his theory that this clause would prevent relatives in-heriting perhaps quite substantial amounts when they had really done nothing for their relatives in Kincarrathie.

On 24 July 1970, William Govan Farquharson, M.C., LL.D., C.A., received the Freedom of the City of Perth, thus following the man who gave him his chance, Arthur Kinmond Bell. Between A.K.'s Freedom in 1938 and Farquie's in 1970, Perth's greatest honour had been bestowed on H.M. the Queen on behalf of the Black Watch (Royal Highland Regiment), Field Marshal Earl Wavell, the Right Hon. Winston Leonard Spencer Churchill and the Right Hon. Sir Anthony Eden, so the two men from Bell's were in good company.

On 5 April 1973, Farquie, as he was affectionately known to the end, died in Perth. He lived long enough to see the profit of Arthur Bell and Sons, Ltd, which he had never imagined would reach £1,000,000, go up to well over £3,000,000. In his time the whole way of the world changed completely. He survived two world wars and all sorts of victories and vicissitudes in the whisky trade.

Explosion!

How do you describe an explosion? For that's what took place in the douce, easy-going firm of Arthur Bell and Sons, Ltd, Perth. After 145 years of getting on nicely, with occasional worries, to be sure, but nothing that couldn't be got over, they suddenly went into five years of fireworks, bangs and brilliant illuminations. They went up like a rocket but, unlike the average rocket, they keep going up.

Now, at the risk of offending Raymond C. Miquel, I have got to say that he was responsible. I have had the privilege of being allowed to write this book as I please, a privilege not often given to authors of this type of work. So I am taking advantage of that privilege to say that the striking success of Bell's over the last five years has been due to the fact that Raymond Miquel laid the train of gunpowder and struck the match which started the explosion.

He started laying the train when he was appointed deputy managing director in 1965. At that time he realized that an infusion of public money was necessary for Bell's to develop their potential. 'But it took me four years to convince the rest of the Board of Directors that this was necessary.' By this time progress in every field, particularly including such facilities for extra production as the new plant at East Mains in West Lothian, started to snowball. Yes, I know that snowballs shouldn't really enter into an explosion, but I hope you will get my drift!

Raymond Miquel became managing director of Bell's in 1968. He became deputy chairman as well as managing director in 1972, and in 1973, as I have recorded, he took over the top position of chairman and managing director on the death of W. G. Farquharson. He spent much of his time building a strong team around him and encouraging those who work for Bell's. Now he was able to display his talents for organization, and he sometimes recalled the time when he produced Bell's first organization chart to the bewilderment and, it must be admitted, the amusement in some cases, of the directors.

Long before he prepared that organization chart, Raymond Miquel had written a thesis entitled 'The Effect of Industrial Engineering Techniques on the Scotch Whisky Industry', based on his experiences at the Bell's warehouse in Leith. It makes quite remarkable reading nowadays, and perhaps the outstanding point is that it is not just time and motion study, but a paper with a very strong realization of human nature and the importance of the worker on the floor. Just to give one simple instance, in his work study project in Leith, he noticed right away that the main door to the bottling plant was so situated that there was a permanent draught blowing on the workers. This, he thought, was the reason for so much minor illness among them. So one of the first points he made was that provision should be effected to exclude the draught.

Bell's has been described as a pacemaker in the Scotch whisky industry, and it is easy to see why. They are always looking for new business and production methods. They were among the first of the Scotch whisky firms to introduce a computerized accounting system for whisky stocks. This, it may surprise some of the 'traditionalists' to know, helps to keep Bell's various blends at the high standard that they have maintained for years. The Bell's policy is to keep big stocks of maturing whiskies for blending in the future, and the recording of these stocks was transferred some years ago from a manually recorded system to a computer bank, so that at any moment the whereabouts of a particular mature single malt can be discovered at once. If you're just a whisky drinker, and not a whisky producer, this may not seem all that important to you. Well, I'm not daft on computers myself, but I've seen the good work this system has done for Bell's in ensuring the quality that was so important to Arthur Bell in the early days.

But, to continue with the pleasant idea of Bell's as a pacemaker in the Scotch whisky industry, let's take the year of 1970. The Scotch industry in that particular year had an average increase of 20 per cent in their export trade. For the same year Bell's export trade was increased by no less than 52 per cent. They shipped whisky to more

The bottling plant at East Mains

than a hundred countries, and they were among the top ten selling Scotch whiskies in South Africa, Russia, Germany, Japan, Italy, Singapore, Spain, Australia, New Zealand and the Channel Islands.

It's been known for years, of course, that Bell's is by far the most popular whisky on its native heath, and independent surveys taken in 1971 and 1975 revealed that 34 per cent of all Scotch whisky drinkers in Scotland who actually demanded a brand by name asked for Bell's.

As far as their three distilleries, Dufftown-Glenlivet, Inchgower and Blair Athol were concerned, it was reported in 1970 that the annual output of single malt whiskies had risen in ten years from some 400,000 proof gallons to well over 2,000,000.

Year by year the firm seems to get bigger and better and produce more and more bewildering statistics. The report for the year 1973 showed a record profit for the company of £4,033,000. Home sales of whisky had more than trebled in six years. Export sales were more than doubled.

In the report of 1973 a final and very important point would certainly have appealed to the original Arthur Bell who, you may remember, was very preoccupied with bottles. In 1973 there was a difficult supply situation in Britain as far as glass bottles were concerned, and Bell's had been forced to deal with overseas bottle-manufacturing firms. They solved that problem by acquiring 'a significant investment' in Canning Town Glass Works, Ltd, who were the largest suppliers of bottles to Bell's. The chairman of Bell's was invited to become chairman of the board of Canning Town Glass Works. Now the glass works are owned entirely by Bell's.

If you want proof of the Bell's explosion, all you have to do is look at the statistics published in 1976 for the previous six years. They showed that Bell's distilleries' output had gone up from 1,830,000 proof gallons in 1970 to 3,870,000 proof gallons in 1974. Bottling had increased during the same period from 1,510,000 dozens to 4,020,000 dozens.

Home sales of Bell's whisky rose from £18,800,000 in 1970 to £65,570,000 in 1975. Export sales went up from £3,050,000 to £7,270,000. Trading profit increased in those years from £1,580,000 to £7,190,000, and during the same period assets increased from £15·67 million to £57·49 million.

Figures are very important, but seeing things for oneself is just as important. I have been fortunate enough to tour all Bell's distilleries and some of their other plants and have been suitably blinded with science by the charming people who run them. I have already described the three distilleries, Blair Athol, Inchgower and Duff-town-Glenlivet. But I have also visited the new one, Pittyvaich-Glenlivet, just up the road from the old Dufftown-Glenlivet distillery. You could hardly find a bigger contrast.

Dufftown-Glenlivet is low down in a narrow glen. Pittyvaich-Glenlivet is on top of a hill. Dufftown-Glenlivet in its original form was a make-do-and-mend job on the meal and saw mills which already existed there. Most distilleries in Scotland were built first and equipped afterwards. Bell's think that Pittyvaich-Glenlivet is the first to be built the other way round. In other words, they started with the plant and then built the outside of the distillery round it. It's significant, too, that the manager of Pittyvaich-Glenlivet is not a whisky-maker by profession but an engineer. (Much shaking of heads by traditionalists.)

The buildings at Pittyvaich are ultra-modern, so that they bear little resemblance, if any, to the kind of distillery you see along Speyside. But, looking out of one of the big windows of the still room, I saw over on the top of a hill opposite a line of deer come slowly along the skyline.

'Well,' I said to the manager, 'however modern you feel inside this building, all you've got to do is to look out of the window and you'll know you're still in the heart of the Highlands.'

He smiled and shook his head. 'No,' he said, 'I'm afraid not. We're still working here and there's going to be a high building between this window and the deer in a few months.'

The ultra-modern Pittyvaich-Glenlivet distillery

All the same, in spite of all the modernity, one part of Pittyvaich-Glenlivet is exactly the same as Dufftown-Glenlivet. The stills are exact replicas of the stills down the hill. Whatever changes in distilleries, the stills remain the same. And this is not traditional superstition, but good sense.

What impressed me most about Pittyvaich was the space and the cleanliness. Most distilleries I have visited in Scotland have been clean, but few have been spacious. Pittyvaich has a capacity of a million proof gallons a year, and the experts are already pleased with the whisky that the new distillery is producing. There are those who say, of course, that there is no such thing as bad Scotch whisky – just that some whiskies are better than others. Judging by the single malts which Bell's produce in their three other distilleries, Pittyvaich-Glenlivet should make a name for itself too.

Not far from Pittyvaich distillery there is the Distillers By-Products Plant. This will deal with effluent from the company's northern distilleries. The effluent is made into what are called Distillers Dark Grains, which are excellent feeding stuff for cattle.

Bell's have five bonded warehouses in Scotland – the oldest one at Auchtermuchty, the Jimmy Shand country; Dunfermline; Halbeath in Fife; Perth; and East Mains. Dunfermline and Perth also have bottling halls, and East Mains combines bottling with blending (see plates VIII and IX). East Mains, though it's so much bigger than the others, might be said to set the pattern. It has to be seen to be believed – twenty-four acres of modern buildings, worked out, in essence, on the same lines that young Raymond Miquel laid down years ago in his précis on engineering technique applied to the production of whisky. Just to tour the place is a test of your walking ability.

Of some 500 Bell's workers, just over half of them operate at East Mains. In the bottling hall the main feature, to an untutored eye, is a row of what appear to be miniature helter-skelters, as in a fairground. Down them come the cases which are to be filled with bottles. You can't help thinking of the contrast with the miserable conditions at the Leith warehouse – the 'dungeons' – when the young work study engineer first saw the place.

And so, perhaps, we should have a closer look at the fourth man the hour has brought forth for Bell's. Arthur Bell, Arthur Kinmond Bell, and even William Govan Farquharson were men who avoided publicity at all costs. This was the way of things in their day. A.K.,

Bell's advertising for the 1970s (1)

if a Scotsman swallows his pride...

it's
BELL'S

ARTHUR BELL & SONS LTD., Estd. 1825—One of the few INDEPENDENT Companies left in the Scotch Whisky Industry

BELL'S
SCOTCH WHISKY

"Afore ye go"

BELL'S
Old Scotch Whisky

ARTHUR BELL & SONS LTD., Estd. 1825–One of the few INDEPENDENT Companies left in the Scotch Whisky Industry

Bell's advertising for the 1970s (2)

for example, would happily write letters to the newspapers, but he would have shied away from any suggestion that he should be interviewed on a personal basis. Things are different now. What trendy people call the media have taken over, and if you are in big business you must be prepared to face reporters, interviewers, magazine article writers, television and radio men and women, and even chaps who want to write books.

This, I think, is part of the success of Raymond Miquel. He is an outgoing man and he speaks freely to the people who ask him questions. After all, he has nothing to hide. He runs an amazingly successful business, so why shouldn't he talk about it and explain, in the bygoing, what makes him tick.

Here is the Miquel philosophy, as quoted in the Press.

'The only way for Britain to get rid of its problems is for companies to come out of their shells and work harder at whatever they are doing. It's no good saying these are troubled times. We all know that. Forget it, and get out there and do your job.'

Then there's the Miquel understatement of the century – 'I've always had a lot of energy to do things.'

And here are three aphorisms –

'Don't talk about what the competition is doing. Just sell your own product.'

'Fix the price for the product as competitive as possible, and then stick to it.'

'Forget what happened yesterday. Think about today or, even better, tomorrow.'

There is a fourth, which seems to me the most important one, and to sum up what Raymond Miquel thinks about life in Bell's – 'People are the organization.'

Bell's advertising has been, in his time at least, very down-to-earth indeed. It's general in the whisky trade to worry about two things – the restrictions on advertising and the selling of bulk whisky to Japan. This is not the blended Scotch whisky, but the single malts. The Japanese take these malts, add their own kind of whisky and compete with the Scotch whisky trade.

Raymond Miquel wraps up both problems in a single sentence. 'Our advertising,' he says, 'has never relied on glamorous people sipping their Scotch in glossy settings, and we don't sell bulk malt to Japan.'

He is strong on discipline. 'I mean self-discipline. You have two alternatives when it comes to business. If I get an unexpected call from an overseas customer just as I'm going home late on Friday night, I can say one of two things – "Do I go home and play golf, or do I go and meet that unexpected customer?" ' That kind of problem, however, doesn't always arise and his motto, provided nothing unexpected occurs, is 'Week-ends are sacrosanct'.

When it comes to the married life of a super-successful business man, Raymond Miquel rather reminds me of Sir James M. Barrie in his play, *What Every Woman Knows*. Barrie made it plain that behind every successful man there was an understanding woman. Raymond Miquel puts it in a different way. 'Certainly,' he says, 'a wife can understand an ambitious man. But you cannot expect wives to understand business.'

When it comes to the future of Arthur Bell and Sons, Ltd, he is quite uncompromising. 'We have an odd situation in that we have to lay down stocks now for five years ahead, and that needs capital.

'We also need to keep the company moving with the development of new production premises just as we have over the last few years. We could just abandon our plans and become the darlings of the City of London. No development costs would mean bigger profit margins and higher share prices. But we can't work that way.

'We insist that there is going to be a future for this industry and particularly for this company.'

And one thing Raymond Miquel has said to me is – 'I have had to fight to develop this company, and I have learned one important rule – never accept second best.'

If all this makes him seem ruthless, I have given the wrong impression. He is absorbed in the story of Bell's. He is delighted to meet elderly men who have spent their lives in the service of the company and have good stories to tell. Naturally, he never met A. K. Bell but he talks about him as if they had been close together, as I think they are in mind. He has good and bad memories of Farquie, but the good ones predominate.

Once, after a long conversation about the old days and the old ways, he said, 'We brought Bell's into the modern world and changed their whole way of life. But sometimes I've asked myself "Did we destroy something beautiful?" '

And then he went back to work, intent on just one thing – to make Bell's the best.

VIII   The blending and bottling complex at East Mains

IX   Bell's bottling hall at Dunfermline

x   Bell's head office at Cherrybank, Perth

XI   Raymond C. Miquel, chairman and managing
director of Bell's, 'nosing' the product

Happy Birthday

It took four men to carry Bell's birthday cake into the Albany Hotel in Glasgow on the last night of February 1975. It had been specially baked in the city, weighed something over a hundredweight, and was in the shape of a bell. There was a single candle on it, but there should have been 150, for this was the dinner to celebrate Bell's 150th anniversary.

More than 500 people were at the dinner, and they came from all the Bell's plants and offices in Scotland. The Master of Ceremonies was the redoubtable ex-Regimental Sergeant Major Ronald Brittain, for years now the bellringer of Bell's. I remember him best on an occasion at Blair Athol Distillery at Pitlochry, when the Scottish Press were there to see how whisky was made. When it came to the time for leaving the distillery and going up the road to the hospitality suite, the Sergeant Major mustered the journalists into a drill squad, gave them a few sharp words of command, and had them marching along like Scots Guardsmen – well, nearly!

At the Albany the dinner was preceded by the showing of the company film, *A Proud Heritage*, which you could be forgiven for thinking was a fine coloured tribute to the country of Scotland, until you remember afterwards how many times you saw a Bell's vehicle! This film was written and directed by Raymond Miquel, and it is unusual, to say the least, among films of this sort, because it is always being brought up to date. I was a script-writer in the Army Kinematograph Service during the war, along with Peter Ustinov and Eric Ambler, and I know something of the technique. I've heard of films being remade, but this is the first one I've known that keeps abreast of its own times.

I

R.S.M. Ronald Brittain

After the dinner Raymond Miquel proposed the toast of Arthur Bell and Sons, Ltd, and said that it was the first time in history that they had brought together all the units of the company – from Inchgower, Dufftown, Pitlochry, Perth and East Mains, and also salesmen from home and overseas. 'I believe a company is only as good as the people who work for it,' he went on, 'and as a team we work like a well-oiled machine.'

Most of his guests had been involved in the recent developments of Arthur Bell and Sons, which had seen sales increase from 18 million bottles in 1970 to 45 million bottles in 1974. For many years Bell's had been the largest selling whisky in Scotland, and was now among the leaders in several overseas markets.

Raymond Miquel cuts Bell's 150th anniversary cake during the celebration dinner held at the Albany hotel, Glasgow in February 1975

He thanked Bell's employees for their commitment, loyalty and sacrifice, which had led to the firm's spectacular growth, and emphasized their belief that service to the customers was of paramount importance. 'We consider,' he said, 'that with your help we have established Arthur Bell and Sons as the leading independent company in the industry. Our success can be attributed to the quality of Bell's the product, and the quality of Bell's employees.

'With these factors in our favour, we can look forward to the future with confidence and start planning for our 200th years' celebration in 50 years' time. I am sure I shall attend either as a retired employee . . . or invisible and wearing wings!'

He mentioned that they were honoured to have fifteen retired Bell's employees at the celebration and their total service amounted to 388 years. At the top table was David Smart, manager of Blair Athol Distillery, who has by no means retired but has been with Bell's for forty-seven years. Jenny and Georgina Hill, who have already been mentioned in these pages, were also at the top table and marvelled at the difference between their comparatively modest hundredth celebration of Bell's in Glasgow in 1925.

Some of the people present remembered a previous film about Bell's made on W. G. Farquharson's orders some time after the Second World War. It was a pioneer affair set beside *A Proud Heritage* and it was made on a small budget. Bill Meiklejohn, who has been connected with Bell's advertising for many years, helped to make it and when a scene in the Highlands was being filmed and the director thought it could be improved by some Highland mist, it **was** Bill Meiklejohn who lit a cigarette and allowed the smoke to drift across the camera lens! I have seen the old film and can testify that the cigarette smoke looks very like Highland mist indeed.

The 150th Anniversary Dinner was a great successs and set people talking about the Bell's they knew. Inevitably conversation turned among the older ones to the famous A.K. and his Gannochy Trust. I don't know of anything quite like the Gannochy Trust in Scotland, although it is rather like the Carlsberg Trust in Copenhagen. The Danish brewery firm help their city and their country in all sorts of ways, and it was A.K.'s ambition that his Gannochy Trust would do much for Perth.

He founded his Trust in 1937 and in 1941 set aside a considerable part of his own shareholding in Arthur Bell and Sons, Ltd, to be applied in helping the people of Perth and certain parts of Perthshire. As I have recorded, he had already built the Gannochy Housing Estate and paid for it himself. He took a great pride in Gannochy and it was said that he ordered all the hedges surrounding the bungalows and cottages to be trimmed to a certain height, so that he could look over the top and see that all was in order!

Some years ago it became necessary for the Trust to seek permission to extend the terms of its liberality to include the whole of Scotland, and this was granted in 1967.

It would take a book of this size to record all the good work that

**The Bell's Sports Centre, gifted by the Gannochy
Trust to the City of Perth**

has been done by the Gannochy Trust, for it has never been for-
gotten that A. K. Bell's wish was to help ordinary folk. But there
have been big projects too. If you recall the letter that A.K. wrote
to the *Perthshire Advertiser* about the sewage running into the
river Tay, you'll be intrigued to know that the Gannochy Trust has
given considerably more than £600,000 for a new sewage system for
the City of Perth.

The most outstanding example of the Gannochy Trust's operations is to be seen on the North Inch at Perth. It's the Bell's Sports
Centre, a dome-like building which contains facilities for all the
indoor sports – although I must admit that the last time I visited
the Sports Centre they were even practising archery, which I would
have said was an outdoor sport. Bell's Sports Centre, which is a
great amenity for Perth, cost the Gannochy Trust £225,000.

A. K. Bell's home, Kincarrathie House, was extended and

turned into a home for elderly people. I have mentioned W. G. Farquharson's special interest in Kincarrathie, and I can testify that it is a delightful place to visit.

Outside Perth, the Gannochy Trust has provided an eighty-bedroom hall of residence at St Andrews University at a cost of £125,000, a sports pavilion for the young Stirling University for £100,000, and has made a donation of £50,000 for playing fields for the new University of Strathclyde in Glasgow.

The young, the aged, the infirm, have all benefited from the Gannochy Trust, and so has medical research. Indeed, one could say that Arthur Kinmond Bell builded better than he knew.

Quite apart from the Gannochy Trust's interest in Bell's Sports Centre in Perth, the firm itself is closely connected with sporting activities, as befits an organization whose chairman and managing director has run up to the top of Ben Nevis and back. Bell's support many activities in the Perth Sports Centre, especially on competitions for young people.

In the wider field they have the much discussed Football Manager of the Year Award. This, of course, is a promotional effort and a brilliant idea from that point of view. Football fans are wildly patriotic about their teams and, if their manager gets the Bell's Award, it's almost as important as winning the Cup.

There is a Manager of the Month competition as well, and in this case a manager is chosen each month from all four divisions of the English Football League. The prize for each of the four fortunate men is a gallon bottle of Bell's whisky. From them is selected the Manager of the Year, to whom Raymond Miquel presents a cheque for £1000 at a luncheon held the day before the annual Scotland v. England international match. Then the trophy itself is presented by Mr Miquel to the winner just before his club's first home game of the following season.

Then there's the Bell's Scotch Whisky Sailing Barge, which voyages all round the South of England and is tremendously popular everywhere it appears. It has made only one appearance in Scotland, but nobody saw it! The occasion was the opening of the Forth Road Bridge by Her Majesty the Queen. Fog descended and the ceremony was seen through a glass darkly. So was Bell's Scotch Whisky Sailing Barge.

It's a pity we haven't seen more of the boat in Scotland, because there seems to be quite a bit of fun and games connected with the Sailing Barge. Spirits are sometimes high aboard the vessel and the

Bell's Scotch Whisky sailing barge

occasion is recorded when one happy chap fell over the side of the barge into the water. One of Bell's sales representatives gallantly decided to go to his rescue. He dived in, only to discover that he'd dived into one foot of water and nearly stunned himself. The original faller-in was rescued, and the rescuer had to be pulled out of the mud.

Bell's believe in keeping the flag flying, and I turn to the place where the wizards of Bell's weave their spells – the headquarters of the firm at Cherrybank, a charming suburb of Perth (see plate X). Bell's is one whisky firm which does not believe in having its headquarters in London.

The new head offices are a far cry indeed from the well-loved but rather sombre headquarters in Victoria Street. The new building is on a hill, with a golf course on one side (it's a remarkable fact that almost all of Bell's buildings are adjacent to golf courses) and a pleasant suburb on the other. Between the office and this suburb is the Glasgow Road and down the hill the grounds are landscaped, with a tiny loch at the roadside.

I've said Bell's keep the flag flying and there are always at least three flags flying in front of the head office entrance. One is the Saltire of Scotland, one is Bell's own house flag, and the third is the flag of the country whose visitors are paying a call that day. Bell's have a good supply of dozens of flags, but sometimes a country comes along that is not in their flag locker. But there is no reason to worry. They just get in touch with Edinburgh Castle, where, apparently, the flags of all the world have to be kept in case of necessity. The Castle says yes, Bell's collect the flag, and the visitor, when he comes up the drive, beams with delight to see this tribute to his country.

There are some unusual things about this head office. First of all, every member of the staff gets free transport from the town centre to Cherrybank and back again at the end of the day. Second, the staff themselves have agreed to have a lunch-hour which is only half-an-hour. They eat well in a pleasant restaurant, and all meals are free. Is there a snag somewhere? There must be! Well, there is a no-smoking rule for one thing. And for another, the girls are not allowed to wear trousers. Oh, yes, and Bell's Sports Centre doesn't sell strong drink, not even Bell's.

All these rules apply just as much when you go up to the executive office on the top floor. Here you walk into luxurious rooms, beauti-

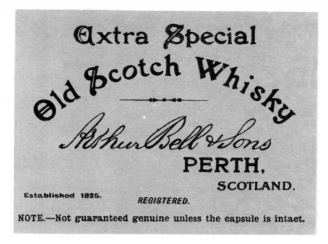

The old and the new. *Top*, one of Bell's first labels, issued in 1904, and *bottom* their current label

fully fitted and furnished. There are three super-secretaries to look after the directors. There is no such thing as a secretary to each director. The secretaries work just as long hours as the directors do and appear to enjoy it.

There are some odd decorations around – in particular, a Japanese samurai warrior's helmet, which was brought to Perth by the President of Bell's Japanese agents to honour the firm's 150 years of existence. There are bells of all kinds. In one room I counted forty-one of them. And there is even a small puzzling piece of paper covered with what seem to be Chinese hieroglyphics and the heading, 'Confucius he says . . .' If you fold it the right way, the hieroglyphics come out clearly as 'Bell's Whisky'.

I mention these small things because they show that the Bell's of today, despite its emphasis on efficiency and progress, is a human place too. The original Arthur Bell might find it a bit bewildering, but I'm sure that A. K. Bell would feel quite at home. Indeed, I can imagine, if Raymond Miquel envisages returning to the Bell's scene in spirit, that A. K. Bell might make a similar phantasmic visit to Cherrybank. And what I feel he would say as he looked around the place is, 'Well, why didn't I think of that?'

And what would the great A.K. think of one of his successors, Raymond Miquel? Well first of all, he'd have some pleasure in knowing that his traditions of service are still being carried on. In 1971–2 Raymond Miquel was chairman of the Scottish Licensed Trade Association. He has already accepted office as the 1976 President of the Licensed Victuallers National Homes, a national charity which has provided nearly five hundred homes for retired licensees. When Raymond Miquel accepted the invitation to be President he said, 'I note that in the 151 years' history of the L.V.N.H., this is only the second time that a company from the Scotch Whisky Industry has been asked to provide a President. I should, therefore, like to thank you for the compliment you have paid to Arthur Bell and Sons Limited and say how honoured I am to be the Company's chosen representative.'

The spirit of A.K. would be pleased too. But he'd also be amazed at his successor's girdling of the world. You'll remember that A. K. Bell, and Farquie after him, spent three months at a time travelling to foreign parts in search of business. What took A.K. three months, Raymond Miquel recently accomplished in three weeks. During that time he visited Hong Kong, Tokyo, Hawaii, Los Angeles, San

Francisco, Chicago, Detroit and New York, and on his return he wrote more than 110 letters to the contacts he made on his trip.

Would the spirit of A. K. Bell grasp that? I think he would. I think he might even be jealous.

ARTHUR BELL AND SONS LIMITED

SCOTCH WHISKY DISTILLERS

ORGANISATION STRUCTURE

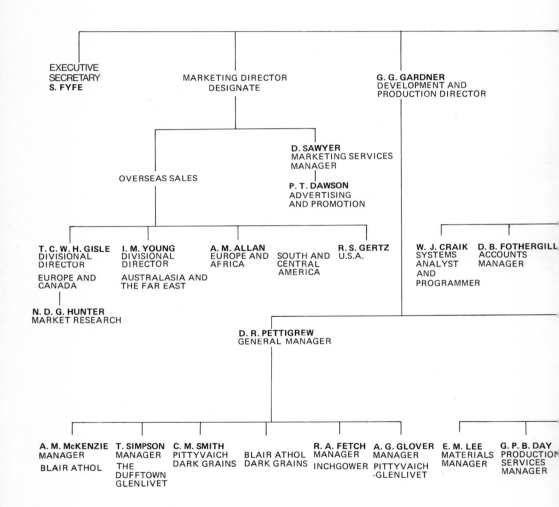

EXECUTIVE SECRETARY
S. FYFE

MARKETING DIRECTOR DESIGNATE

G. G. GARDNER
DEVELOPMENT AND PRODUCTION DIRECTOR

D. SAWYER
MARKETING SERVICES MANAGER

OVERSEAS SALES

P. T. DAWSON
ADVERTISING AND PROMOTION

T. C. W. H. GISLE
DIVISIONAL DIRECTOR
EUROPE AND CANADA

I. M. YOUNG
DIVISIONAL DIRECTOR
AUSTRALASIA AND THE FAR EAST

A. M. ALLAN
EUROPE AND AFRICA

SOUTH AND CENTRAL AMERICA

R. S. GERTZ
U.S.A.

W. J. CRAIK
SYSTEMS ANALYST AND PROGRAMMER

D. B. FOTHERGILL
ACCOUNTS MANAGER

N. D. G. HUNTER
MARKET RESEARCH

D. R. PETTIGREW
GENERAL MANAGER

A. M. McKENZIE
MANAGER
BLAIR ATHOL

T. SIMPSON
MANAGER
THE DUFFTOWN GLENLIVET

C. M. SMITH
PITTYVAICH DARK GRAINS

BLAIR ATHOL DARK GRAINS

R. A. FETCH
MANAGER
INCHGOWER

A. G. GLOVER
MANAGER
PITTYVAICH -GLENLIVET

E. M. LEE
MATERIALS MANAGER

G. P. B. DAY
PRODUCTION SERVICES MANAGER

SUBSIDIARY COMPANIES:

CANNING TOWN GLASS CO., LTD.
TOWMASTER TRANSPORT CO., LTD.
P. MACKENZIE AND CO., DISTILLERS, LTD.
C. AND J. McDONALD, LTD.

FORBES, FARQUHARSON AND CO., LTD.
THE ATHOLL DISTILLERIES LTD.
BURN BRAE (BLENDERS) LTD.

DISTILLERIES:

THE DUFFTOWN-GLENLIVET, DUFFTOWN.
BLAIR ATHOL, PITLOCHRY.
INCHGOWER, BANFFSHIRE.
PITTYVAICH-GLENLIVET, DUFFTOWN.

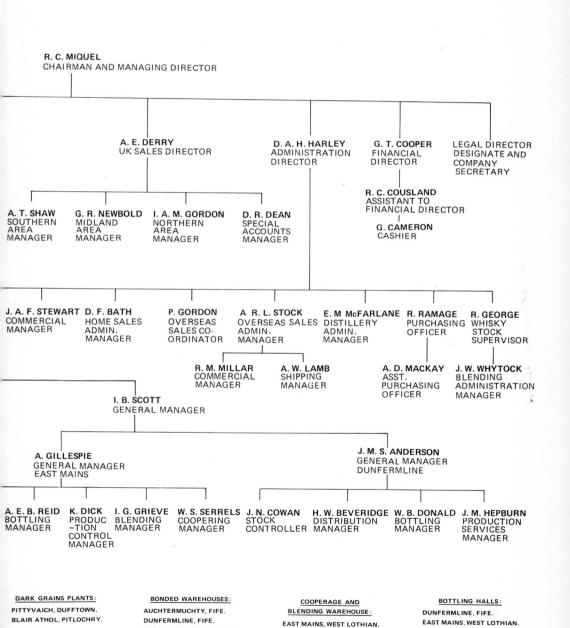

R. C. MIQUEL
CHAIRMAN AND MANAGING DIRECTOR

A. E. DERRY
UK SALES DIRECTOR

D. A. H. HARLEY
ADMINISTRATION
DIRECTOR

G. T. COOPER
FINANCIAL
DIRECTOR

LEGAL DIRECTOR
DESIGNATE AND
COMPANY
SECRETARY

R. C. COUSLAND
ASSISTANT TO
FINANCIAL DIRECTOR

G. CAMERON
CASHIER

A. T. SHAW
SOUTHERN
AREA
MANAGER

G. R. NEWBOLD
MIDLAND
AREA
MANAGER

I. A. M. GORDON
NORTHERN
AREA
MANAGER

D. R. DEAN
SPECIAL
ACCOUNTS
MANAGER

J. A. F. STEWART
COMMERCIAL
MANAGER

D. F. BATH
HOME SALES
ADMIN.
MANAGER

P. GORDON
OVERSEAS
SALES CO-
ORDINATOR

A R. L. STOCK
OVERSEAS SALES
ADMIN.
MANAGER

E. M McFARLANE
DISTILLERY
ADMIN.
MANAGER

R. RAMAGE
PURCHASING
OFFICER

R. GEORGE
WHISKY
STOCK
SUPERVISOR

R. M. MILLAR
COMMERCIAL
MANAGER

A. W. LAMB
SHIPPING
MANAGER

A. D. MACKAY
ASST.
PURCHASING
OFFICER

J. W. WHYTOCK
BLENDING
ADMINISTRATION
MANAGER

I. B. SCOTT
GENERAL MANAGER

A. GILLESPIE
GENERAL MANAGER
EAST MAINS

J. M. S. ANDERSON
GENERAL MANAGER
DUNFERMLINE

A. E. B. REID
BOTTLING
MANAGER

K. DICK
PRODUC
–TION
CONTROL
MANAGER

I. G. GRIEVE
BLENDING
MANAGER

W. S. SERRELS
COOPERING
MANAGER

J. N. COWAN
STOCK
CONTROLLER

H. W. BEVERIDGE
DISTRIBUTION
MANAGER

W. B. DONALD
BOTTLING
MANAGER

J. M. HEPBURN
PRODUCTION
SERVICES
MANAGER

DARK GRAINS PLANTS:
PITTYVAICH, DUFFTOWN.
BLAIR ATHOL, PITLOCHRY.

BONDED WAREHOUSES:
AUCHTERMUCHTY, FIFE.
DUNFERMLINE, FIFE.
EAST MAINS, WEST LOTHIAN.
HALBEATH, FIFE.
PERTH.

COOPERAGE AND
BLENDING WAREHOUSE:
EAST MAINS, WEST LOTHIAN.

BOTTLING HALLS:
DUNFERMLINE, FIFE.
EAST MAINS, WEST LOTHIAN.

LIST OF BELL'S DIRECTORS

ARTHUR BELL	1845–1900
A. THOMPSON	1890–1939
A. K. BELL	1895–1942
ROBIN BELL	1896–1942
D. F. FORBES	1904–1943
D. MACKAY	1922–1949
D. A. AINSLIE	1922–1956
A. T. SUTHERLAND	1922-1972
W. F. FARQUHARSON	1923–1973
Chairman	1942–1973
Managing director	1942–1968
W. MILLER	1925-1969
D. F. CRICHTON	1926–1958
J. G. URE	1948–1976
J. A. R. MACPHAIL	1950–1962
R. C. MIQUEL	1956–
Chairman	1973–
Managing director	1968–
T. DUNCANSON	1958–1975
D. A. H. HARLEY	1958–
G. G. GARDNER	1959–
W. L. GEDDES	1960–1967
G. T. COOPER	1969–
A. E. DERRY	1969–
K. A. GRAHAM	1971–1974

Acknowledgments for Illustrations

Page 4 Perth from the South, showing pumping station (round tower), now the Tourist Information Board.
Perth Art Gallery and Museum

Page 5 The Very Revd Theobald Matthew, Temperance reformer.
Radio Times Hulton Picture Library

Page 9 Excise duty, 1723. The Mansell Collection

Page 23 The head of Loch Lomond, looking south.
Perth Art Gallery and Museum

Page 31 A. K. Bell, 1899. Perth County Cricket Club

Page 44 Perthshire cricket team, 1909.
Perth County Cricket Club

Page 54 Prohibition in Boston, 1920.
Radio Times Hulton Picture Library

Page 58 'I Want to be Happy' from *No No Nanette*.
Raymond Mander and Joe Mitchenson Theatre Collection

Page 84 Advertisement 'R-R-Resoundingly Fine'.
New York Times, 31 March 1945

Page 94 The Perth–Dundee railway line.
Perth Art Gallery and Museum

All other black and white illustrations courtesy of Arthur Bell and Sons Ltd